Service with a HUG

Because Customers Want to Feel Loved!

Written by Andy Collett

Thirty Ways to Transform Your Customer's Experience

(and Your Own…)

Second edition

ISBN: 9798867779382

Dedicated to my Mum

Phyllis Hobbs

The first person to give me a hug

CONTENTS

Part 3 – 'G' – Guide with Integrity

INTRODUCTION

What Is Service with a HUG All About?

Carol runs her own small business. It's a gift shop in Scotland. She said 'One of my customers told me that when they visit the shop, they feel as if they've been hugged'. I'm talking about creating a feeling - a feeling that keeps customers coming back - an interaction that leaves them feeling better...

When I asked Carol to describe how she achieves that feeling, she thought long and hard and in a seemingly intuitive way just said *it's different for every customer*. Yes, of course! I wanted examples. I drilled down. Eventually, I discovered that she connects with her customers by giving them a warm welcome and simply asking them how they are today (and really meaning it). Rocket science? I think not. Powerful? Incredibly so.

Why Did I Write This Book?

Because I am passionate about customer service. For the past 20+ years my business has specialised in training and coaching front-line staff and their managers, to create an amazing experience for their customers. I get a huge buzz out of seeing customers having a great time - seeing them smiling, laughing and spreading the word. As a customer myself, I enjoy being on the receiving end of great service, and I'm always quick to praise those who 'get it' and give it.

How Can This Book Help You?

Let me answer that question with a question. What made you choose this book? Write down your answer on the next page. That way, as you read, your mind will link the words on the page with your goal or reason. When we have clarity around our goals, it's amazing what can show up. So please, take a moment and do it now; it's important.

....
....
....
....
....
....
....
....
....
....
....
....
....
....
....

OK, so now you've done that, let me ask, what that will give you? Write that down too.

....
....
....
....
....
....
....
....
....
....
....
....
....

PART 1
HANDLE SKILFULLY

Any intelligent fool can make things bigger, more complex and more violent. It takes a touch of genius – and a lot of courage – to move in the opposite direction.

Albert Einstein

What I have found when studying people who are really successful - in whatever field - is that they tend to keep things simple by mastering the fundamentals rather than making things more complicated.

The other key factor is how exceptionally well they work with those around them – their colleagues and suppliers. This is a concept we'll expand upon – the idea that there are *internal* customers too. Those who we look to for support and also those who depend upon us.

So Part 1 is all about developing the foundations upon which to build. You could think of it as paying attention to the basic essentials. On its own, this doesn't usually deliver a memorable experience for the customer – although occasionally it can, depending on their level of expectation.

Even though you may feel that some of the concepts in this first part are just plain common sense, if you were to purely apply the ideas suggested in Part 1 you would probably stand out as being ahead of the mainstream. Your customers would really notice and remember you. As was once said 'common sense isn't that common!'.

If you are already familiar with many of these essential elements, I'm sure you'll appreciate the value of re-visiting these primary skills that helped you create the success you've had to date.

However good we are, we can always be better. We can always do more and be more for our customers and benefit ourselves in the process.

So here we go – let's dive in...

1. ACKNOWLEDGE

First impressions matter. Experts say we size up new people in somewhere between 30 seconds and two minutes

Elliott Abrams

It makes sense that we begin by acknowledging our customers. If we don't get the first impression right, we may not have an opportunity to deliver any of the great service that we love providing to our customers.

And acknowledgement needs to be offered, whether meeting a customer face-to-face, on the telephone, replying to an email, or on social media.

It's a cultural thing
In some businesses, for example certain hotels, staff members are trained to acknowledge a customer as they pass in the corridor. As a customer, this feels very nice. And for me, it can be taken much further than this.

- It's not just about doing something because we've been trained to do. It needs to be seen as a core part of our role as a service provider. Something essential that we're proud to do.
- It's not just about acknowledging customers when we pass them in the corridor (nice though that is). We should acknowledge customers whenever we can. Maybe have a bit of a chat to them if the situation allows. After all, it's the customer who is paying our wages!

- This is not just for the people in the business who deal with the customers. This applies to everyone who works in the business, whether front of house or not.
- It's not just about acknowledging *customers*. It's about acknowledging another human being, whether they are a colleague, a maintenance person, a delivery driver, or indeed a customer. This is about creating a friendly, welcoming environment – because that helps everyone!

Create the kind of environment that you would enjoy working in. As Gandhi said, 'Be the change you want to see in the world'.

Face-to-face situations – in our own environment
Acknowledging a customer quickly as they enter our space is essential and we are not talking about 'pouncing' – most customers can feel the 'pushy' energy behind that. We need to acknowledge in a way that is warm, gentle, friendly and sincere.

What are our intentions at this starting point? What are we trying to achieve?

- A positive first impression (see below for more on this)
- To put the customer at ease (they might be a little nervous,
defensive, or closed)
- To establish a connection (see Chapter 2 for more on this)
- To invite a comfortable conversation

Working in an environment where customers enter our premises - for example a retail shop, car showroom or restaurant - how long do customers need to be left alone? It's impossible to generalise as it's going to be different every time. Some customers demand instant attention. Others prefer to be left alone to wander around and get a feel for what's on offer. So, as the service provider, what can we do to get this right for each customer every time?

We've all seen what happens when a customer walks into a shop and meets an assistant who immediately asks 'Can I help you?'. This question often triggers the conditioned response 'No thanks, I'm just looking' - even if they are actually interested in making a purchase! It's important for the service provider not to come across as pushy as the customer can feel swooped upon and they may interpret the question as 'what would you like to buy today?'. The likelihood is it's too early in the process for the customer to feel ready to make a decision.

This is when it's so helpful to have a welcome desk or receptionist as the customer's first point of contact. We can establish the purpose of their visit and provide the appropriate level of assistance. Perhaps they have already spoken with someone and would like to be directed to that person. Perhaps they have an appointment. All very useful to know at this early stage.

The first objective is very simple. Make them feel welcome. That's it!

If a customer is in our shop or showroom, how about just saying hello, introducing ourselves and offering to be available if required? Something like, 'Hello, my name's Amanda. If you need help with anything, just let me know.' Most customers will pick up on the different energy of this approach and begin to let their barriers down.

Carefully observe the body language of customers as they wander around.

- If they start to look around for some assistance, that's our cue

- If they start heading for the door, it's worth asking them if they've found what they were looking for
- If they haven't made a purchase, we may have an opportunity to help them

Face-to-face situations – in the customer's environment
When we are visiting a customer at their workplace or home, once again a warm greeting is in order. 'Hello, I'm David. It's good to meet you' - followed by a little small talk to put them at ease and build trust. Getting straight into business the moment we step through the door – whether it's to give a quotation for fitting a window blind, repairing their computer or washing machine - is equivalent to 'pouncing'.

Small talk might include asking them how their day has been so far or showing interest in something in the room, for example a trophy, or a picture – anything that may have significance. This approach can go too far and have a negative impact if customers feel we've crossed the line in terms of privacy or relevance. So keep it brief and appropriate to the situation. Also, as we move into work mode, be sure to be respectful of the customer's space and time by asking permission: 'Is it OK if I…?' and then make the request.

On the telephone – incoming call
On the telephone, it's not just about answering the call quickly. It's also about how we respect that person's time once we have begun the conversation. We soon get a sense of how the customer is feeling. If they seem rushed or irritated, it's worth checking out how they are fixed for time. They could be calling us during their lunch break. They could have experienced frustrations getting through to speak to us. Acknowledging that, apologising if it feels appropriate, will most likely result in the customer feeling heard and will enable the conversation to proceed on a more positive note compared to us ploughing on regardless. And, of course, if the customer has a particularly

chirpy demeanour, that's worth acknowledging too (probably not using that description though!)

On the telephone – outbound call
For those times when we are making an outbound telephone call, again it's worth acknowledging early on that we may have called at a bad time and asking them if they have time to speak. The customer will appreciate our thoughtfulness and will normally be happy to arrange a more convenient time when we can have a higher quality conversation.

Online – email, social media, SMS, messaging apps, video calls (the list goes on)
When you are communicating using technology, it needs a high degree of awareness. You probably already know how easily misunderstandings can occur.

Why do people use emojis in messages and on social media? Because this is one way to convey the energy, the emotion of the words. Emotion is the component that is present when you are having an in-person conversation and is absent in typed messages. Used with care, emojis can definitely contribute that missing element.

Importantly, with these electronic media methods, there's often a 'tail'. In other words, there's either a written record that can be referred back to or, in the case of video calls (such as Zoom), there can be a recording of the conversation. Or other people could be listening in without you knowing. Best to assume that the whole world will be able to see and hear you.

Therefore, if you don't know who else can read your message or see you on video, slow down! Especially in those situations when you are feeling highly emotional. For example, when someone wants to make a purchase – you're excited! Or the opposite, perhaps they are complaining – you might get defensive. Breathe. Connect with your wisdom. Be curious. Ask questions. Create some thinking time. Focus initially on acknowledging them and their situation.

First Impressions

How quickly is a first impression formed? Many people feel that a first impression is formed in just a few seconds. Once that first impression is made, how easily can it be changed? My experience tells me that it's pretty difficult. Why is that? Well, as human beings, we like to be right about things. We don't like to admit that we may have got it wrong, made a mistake, or been too hasty. So, when we weigh up someone, something, or somewhere and make our judgements, our minds look for evidence to support those judgements. Anything that doesn't fit gets filtered out. It takes an overwhelming amount of evidence to the contrary to make us change our minds.

What's my point?

Firstly, it really is true that we don't get a second chance to make a first impression. It's made and that's it – it is what it is - which means that we need to make a positive first impression to connect with the maximum number of customers. If we don't, customers may not stay around to give us a chance to win them over.

Secondly, when we are busy forming our first impression of a customer, we need to stay open to the possibility that our judgements of them could change. In other words, don't take that first impression as 'truth'. It is just 'a snapshot in time' and may not be at all representative of the whole person.

What are the contributing factors to a first impression?

- **Non-verbal communication** – how people are dressed, personal presentation, grooming, hygiene, facial expression, and body language
- **Tone of voice** – accent, energy, enthusiasm and warmth
- **Language** – the words that are actually spoken!

Out of these three aspects, it's interesting to reflect on which ones have the most impact and which the least:

- Non-verbal communication has the **most** impact when meeting **face-to-face**
- Tone of voice is the **most important** when we are on the **telephone**
- The words have the **least impact** both face-to-face and on the telephone

Surprising? Not really. As human beings, we have an instinctive, intuitive, inner knowing about other people. It reaches back thousands of years to when we needed to assess potential levels of threat - when it was life or death to know if we could trust another person. Yet these instinctive responses are still the most influential factors when we are dealing with others.

So how can we improve our own first impression?

Firstly, we need to gain a sense of the first impression we are currently making. As it's difficult to assess this ourselves, why not try a little test? Next time you meet someone for the first time and if it feels appropriate, ask some of the following questions:

- What was your first impression of me?
- What was it about me that gave you that impression?
- Who do I remind you of and why?
- What did you first notice about me?

- What do you think I could do to make a better first impression?

I would often encourage participants on workshops to ask these questions of each other. It's always delightful to observe them hearing how they come across to others. It can be very different from how they thought and that's great – now they're in a position to do make changes if they want to.

Action tips

- Offer a friendly greeting and acknowledgement every time
- Avoid jumping to conclusions about customers – practice staying neutral and curious
- Ask questions to raise your awareness of the first impression you make
- Be aware that it's **how** you come across that will have the most impact, not what you say

---

2. CONNECT

*The business of business is relationships;
the business of life is human connection.*

Robin S. Sharma

What does it mean to connect with another human being? And why is that important in customer service situations?

We've all experienced being a customer when there was a lack of connection. How was that for you? Normally it's totally forgettable. Or perhaps it was so poor that you decided never to go back, told others, and were even moved to complain to the manager.

Connection is not about being trained to say the right words - that's a bit fake, and customers see through it in an instant. It's more to do with an energy or attitude.

What are you feeling?
The impact of how you feel is sensed by others – your customers and colleagues. If you're going through the motions, not really wanting to be there, what's going on? Do you need a change? A break? A fresh challenge? A different role?

You're not at the mercy of how you feel, although it can seem that way. Often it's the story we are telling ourselves – the perspective we are aligning with, what we are believing to be true – that determines how we feel.

What are you believing?
Breaking news: how it seems to you is not how it is. You get to

experience your stories. Here are some examples:

- Customers waste my time – (yep, they do don't they)
- Nobody's buying at the moment – (so true, and you can prove it)
- Every customer really appreciates me – (that's nice)
- Customers are rude – (you're determined to be right about that)

Notice the stories you're believing and how they play out. If you don't like what's happening, try creating it differently. Notice the story and choose a different one.

How do other people pick up on our stories, our energy?

Eye contact

So much of our connection with others revolves around eye contact. Pretty much everyone will tell you that eye contact is a really important aspect of communication. With great eye contact we come across as more engaged, friendly, and confident. Also, it provides us with a lot of non-verbal information about how the other person is feeling. More on this in Part 2.

Focus

Really connecting with another person telegraphs 'You are the only person I'm interested in at this moment'. That means no side conversations with colleagues, no taking phone calls, or responding to any other kind of distraction. And if we get interrupted, apologise to the customer and ask permission to respond to the interruption. Afterwards, apologise again.

A great resource is the 'Pike Place Fish Video' in which the employees talk about 'Being There' for their customers. The employees entertain and get up close and personal with their customers who love the playful way the team members are selling their produce at a fish stall. Search online if you're curious to find out more.

Smiling

A smile is an invitation. It sends a non-verbal message: 'I am sincere, open, welcoming and interested in assisting you.' If you're not someone who has a naturally smiley face (not everyone is blessed in this way) avoid pretending. Pretend smiles tend to look more like a grimace! Try interacting with customers' pets or family members - if present - which offer great opportunities to produce a smile. Your colleagues can probably help too, through banter and playfulness.

Bring a light-hearted attitude to work. I've heard some people grumbling 'If you worked where I work...' I get it. However, we can choose how our day pans out. Do we want to enjoy our day, or would we rather be miserable? We decide. If we want to enjoy our day, it may take a little effort at the start, but the enjoyment soon gathers momentum - a bit like a snowball.

Customers pick up on energy. When they enter a happy place they feel it and they love it. Just make sure that, if there's laughter going on, we always include the customer in the hilarity, otherwise they might suspect that we're laughing at them!

Rapport

Chapter 12 covers this in more detail. For now, let's just define rapport as 'personal connection with warmth'. There are many ways to achieve a warm connection. Think about some of the ways in which you've created rapport in your life. How about when you're not at work? How do you show those around you that they matter to you? And how do you create a sense of connection with your customers and colleagues?

Jot down what comes to mind and we'll refer back to this in Chapter 12 (Match).

....
....
....
....
....
....
....
....
....
....
....
....
....
....
....
....
....
....
....
....
....
....
....
....

Action tips

- Be aware of how you're feeling and question what you're believing to be true
- Smile and make eye contact
- Connect with your customer in a friendly, relaxed way
- Give others your undivided attention

3. QUESTION

Questions are very powerful. They give us information about the customer and their needs. Plus they help demonstrate professionalism and interest in the customer. They are an investment in the relationship - mostly. It depends on the questions we ask. So, what kinds of questions are most useful? Neutral, open, curious, and well-structured questions. All of this applies to interactions with our colleagues too.

Neutral Questions
These are questions that are not loaded with an agenda. A neutral question might be 'What was it that made you decide to come and see us today?' A loaded question might be 'Was it the great finance deal that made you contact us?' It's obvious where the salesperson wants to take the conversation – they're more interested in selling a finance package than finding out what is important to the customer.

Closed Questions
A closed question is one that has a very limited answer like 'yes' or 'no'.
Closed questions are very restrictive and require work on the part of the person answering to fully get the information across. In some cases, the customer might answer a different question – the one they wish the salesperson had asked. For example, the salesperson may ask 'Have you come in to check out the wide range of colours available?' and the customer may answer 'Partly, but I would also like you to run through all the optional extras that are listed on the website please'.

Open Questions
An open question is an invitation to expand and answer fully. Unlike closed questions, they don't suggest an answer. For example, 'What is important to you in your new kitchen?' is a great open question, perfect just as it is.

Sometimes people will close down a lovely open question by offering a possible response, for example, 'What was it that prompted you contact us today?' (that's a nice neutral, open question that works as it is). Before the customer has a chance to respond, 'Did you see one of our advertisements?' So this is something for you to be alert to.

Open questions typically begin with the following words:

- Who...?
- What...?
- Where...?
- When...?
- Which...?
- How...?

Curious Questions

I'm curious - how many people do you know who are genuinely curious? As a customer, I find that some sales people ignore me or push an agenda or simply recite their spiel. It's really refreshing to interact with a sales person who makes an effort to find out more about me, to discover what advice they can offer, and locate the best product or service to meet my needs. Whenever I encounter service like that, I go back again and again and I recommend them at every opportunity.

Well-Structured Questions

The sequence of the questions makes a big difference. For example, we can ask a question about one topic, thinking that's all there is to know; ask a question about another topic, before moving on to a third! Instead, how about we stay with the first topic and fully explore that before moving on. Being on the receiving end of someone who does this with skill feels simply wonderful. It feels almost therapeutic! Let me give an example.

A customer is interested in buying a new motorcycle. They are interested in comfort, reliability and they want a good-sized fuel tank.

A poor sequence (of really quite good questions) could be:

Salesperson: 'What's important to you in your next bike?'

Customer: 'Comfort'

Salesperson: 'Ah, great. Yes, that's important. What else?' (now making an assumption that they understand what the customer means by comfort)

Customer: 'Big fuel tank'

Salesperson: 'Ah, big fuel tank! Yes! What else?'

Customer: 'Reliability'

Salesperson: 'Of course, we don't want to break down do we...'

You get the idea. The conversation is disjointed, moving quickly from topic to topic. Each topic is not fully explored. The information is taken at face value and the salesperson is applying their own interpretation.

Here's a better version:

Salesperson: 'What's important to you in your next bike?'

Customer: 'Comfort'

Salesperson. 'Ah, OK. When you say comfort, would you mind telling me a little about what you mean by that?'

Customer: 'Sure. The riding position needs to be comfortable, and also I want good protection from the elements.'

Salesperson: 'Thanks for that. Comfortable riding position and good protection from the elements. Tell me, why are those aspects of comfort particularly important to you?'

Customer: 'Well, you see, I cover long distances; on some trips, I can be on the bike for quite a few hours in a day. I need a comfortable riding position and also, because I ride all year round, I need good weather protection.'

Salesperson: 'Wow! That's proper motorcycling! Respect!'

Customer: 'Thanks!'

Salesperson: 'What else is important to you?'

The salesperson spends some time on each topic before moving on to the next.

In this second example, the salesperson is finding out much more about the customer and how they use the bike. Not only that, the questions have a much more conversational flow to them. The customer is likely to feel that the salesperson is taking more interest and being much more thorough.

Action tips

- Ask great questions – it reveals so much and enables us to guide the conversation
- Use predominantly curious, open, neutral questions
- Be aware of the sequence of your questions – fully explore one topic before moving on to the next

---

4. PERSONALISE

Assessing the Customer's Style

There's a commonly used saying that we should treat customers how we would like to be treated. Wrong! We need to treat customers the way *they* would like to be treated. We're not all the same.

Have you noticed that some people buy on impulse, not really thinking it through? Have you noticed that some people like to do lots of research and, even if they find the perfect product within their budget, they still want to go away and think about it?

What if we were to treat the impulsive buyer the way we would a slow, cautious buyer? What would happen? You can imagine the conversation now; the customer, all excited, desperate to get their hands on their shiny new gadget is confronted by a sales person saying 'Well, I guess you'll be wanting to go away and think about it. Here's the sales literature for the one you're interested in - and for the other models - just in case you find you'd rather have one of them.' The customer, meanwhile, is gradually losing the will to live!

Instead, why not ask a few key questions:

- 'What do you need from your visit today?'
- 'How are you fixed for time?'
- 'What's your timescale for making a decision?'
- 'What's the most important factor in choosing your....?'
- 'How much do you already know?'

Tailoring the Experience

Look for opportunities to tailor the customer's experience. For some customers, it's not even about the product itself. It might be the backup service, the resulting relationship and peace of mind that's most important to them.

Don't expect the customer to flex to fit your process. Many retailers think it's their customers' job to do the flexing, but actually *we* are the ones who need to adjust our process and style to make it a great experience for them. After all, customers are responsible for paying our wages!

- If it's an **emotional** buyer, be excited and enthusiastic. Don't give them all the technical details
- If it's a **rational** buyer, focus on the practical, sensible attributes of what it is you offer
- Match their **pace**, slow down if the customer is cautious, speed up if the customer is decisive

What emerges when you combine these factors is four distinctly different ways of being a customer. They are:
- An emotional customer with a slow pace
- An emotional customer with a fast pace
- A rational customer with a slow pace
- A rational customer with a fast pace

Here's how to identify each style and flex to create the ideal experience for the customer – or colleague!

Emotional customer with slow pace

How to identify:
- Gentle
- Caring
- Warm
- Cautious, tentative
- Indecisive
- Tendency to worry
- Relationship is a key factor

How to flex:

- Match their slower pace and gentle style
- Build rapport, get to know them
- Offer guidance and reassurance
- Avoid giving too many options or choices to make
- Help them to get clear on what is most important to them
- Avoid too much in the way of facts and data

Emotional customer with fast pace

How to identify:

- Sociable
- Energetic
- Enthusiastic
- Tactile
- Impulsive
- Relaxed
- Feelings-led

How to flex:

- Match their faster pace and enthusiasm
- Avoid too much in the way of facts and data
- Focus on the emotional aspects of what you offer – how they might feel
- Make every aspect as easy as possible for them – especially them saying 'yes' to what you are offering

A rational customer with a slow pace

How to identify:

- Cautious
- Reserved
- Quietly spoken
- Precise

- Formal
- Loves to plan ahead
- Takes longer to make a decision
- Bases decisions on facts and data

How to flex:

- Match their slower pace and reserved style
- Avoid personal questions – stick to what is relevant
- Provide all the facts and data they need
- Give them plenty of personal space – both physically and in terms of time to think
- Help them to weigh up all the options
- Let them know why this might be a good time to make the purchase
- Definitely avoid anything that they may experience as pressure or 'sales talk'

A rational customer with a fast pace

How to identify:

- Competitive
- Purposeful
- Outspoken
- Results-driven
- Confident
- Direct

How to flex:

- Match their faster pace and confidence
- Provide the facts and data they need – just top-level
- Avoid personal questions – stick to what is relevant
- Acknowledge their success or achievements
- Talk about what is possible rather than what is not
- Create for them a feeling of winning, especially during negotiations

You may find this a little challenging at first (or you may not). Either way, you'll find it gets easier and easier the more you do it, to the point where you're not even thinking about it. Eventually, it becomes effortless and natural.

Let's be easy to do business with.

Using the Customer's Name
It's a small, simple, yet incredibly powerful technique and it's a big deal to most people. Using their name says 'you are important to me'. Try it and you'll be astounded by the results. How many times do other service providers use your name in a typical day? It's memorable when it happens. Take care not to over-use it though, as it can become annoying and seem insincere.

Action tips

- Assess the customer's style and adapt to it
- Be flexible with your sales process
- Personalise by occasionally addressing the customer by name

---

5. COMMUNICATE

> ## Communicate (verb)
> *To convey knowledge of or information about.*
> *To make known.*

It's impossible to not communicate. We're doing it all the time. The key consideration is our level of awareness of how and what we are communicating.

To communicate is to 'make known'. What are we making known? And what are we not making known?

Here are some thoughts to consider.

What are we making known?

Very obviously, there's what we say. We use words as our everyday method of communication. Estimates vary in terms of how many words per day we typically use. It could be in the range of 5,000 to 7,000 for many people. Primarily what we are making known is the content – conveying knowledge or information. 'My name is Andy' is an example of conveying information.

It goes much further than that. There's how we speak – our voice tone, energy, emphasis, speed, inflection, enunciation, willingness to pause, etc. All these factors provide additional information about how we see the world and our relationship with it. Whether we are aware of it or not, these are aspects we are making known about ourselves and how we are feeling.

You may know something about non-verbal communication. Included in this category would be our body language, facial expression, eye contact, gestures, appearance, clothes, etc. You may be aware of some ways in which you communicate non-verbally. There may also be aspects of your non-verbal communication that you are yet to discover. This is a massive area to explore; there are many subtleties. Remember, just because something is subtle does not mean it has little impact.

If you choose to expand your awareness of what and how you are communicating to others (and yourself), there is a whole journey awaiting you.

If this sounds interesting to you, my suggestion would be to explore NLP – Neuro Linguistic Programming. For me, learning to become a Master Practitioner of NLP and later a Certified NLP Coach has been a huge contribution to my professional and personal life. One quote from NLP that has stuck with me is 'The meaning of the communication is the response it elicits'. In other words, it's not what you say, it's what they hear that really counts.

What are we not making known?

As a customer or colleague, it's often what we would call the lack of communication that we feel frustrated about.

Someone I was working with once said to me, 'I can deal with bad news. What I find more difficult is being kept in the dark'. And yet, what we would call a lack of communication (at the level of form) is actually still communicating something. We might interpret the apparent lack of communication as uncaring, not being bothered, too busy or something else. It could also be that the person did communicate and we missed it.

When we go somewhere, we keep in touch with our friends and family. 'Here's a picture of a lovely old building in the town square. Here's a picture of where we're having lunch. Here's a picture of lunch. Here's a picture of the empty plate – that was delicious!' It just happens, we don't have to force ourselves to do it. What if it could be this easy with customers and colleagues?

It is. There are so many ways to contact a customer, especially these days. And it's especially relevant when there's something to update a customer about. For example to say, 'I'm pleased to let you know that your order has arrived'. Or perhaps it could be, 'I'm sorry to tell you that there's been a delay'. Either way, you're better off knowing – and crucially, so is the customer. They will appreciate you being proactive, rather than them having to contact you for an update.

More ideas on proactive communication in the next chapter.

Action tips

- Build your awareness of what you are making known and what you are not making known
- Ask yourself 'How might this communication be interpreted by others?'
- Be proactive in your communication with customers and colleagues

6. BE PROACTIVE

Great customer service involves being highly responsive to our customers' needs – whether that's an external customer or an internal one (a colleague). Being proactive is one way to bring that responsiveness to our interactions. What do we mean by being proactive? For me, it means creating change by taking action - fulfilling our customers' desires by taking the initiative.

Being proactive means that we show initiative, think for ourselves and drive the situation forward. For instance, we could say things like, 'Would you like...?', 'You look like you might be...', 'I notice that...', 'Can I... for you?'

The opposite, being reactive, means that we only act in response to a situation in which case nothing happens unless the customer asks for something. For example, 'Can I have...?', Do you have...?', Is there any...?', 'Where can I find...?'. You get the idea.

By taking the initiative we can improve all areas of customer service. Let's look at some ways in which we can be more proactive.

Noticing what is Going On

We need to remember to raise our heads and look around!

- Is there a customer who looks lost or unsure?
  Action - We can check to see if they need help
- Have we noticed a customer waiting for something?
  Action - Perhaps we can speed up the process
- Is there an untidy display?
  Action - Go ahead and tidy the display
- Is there an item without point-of-sale material?
  Action - Add the missing material
- Are there items that aren't priced?
  Action - Go ahead and price them

We know that it's important to **Do What You Say You Will Do** (or DWYSYWD – sounds like a small town in Wales!) When we go beyond that and **Do *More* Than You Say You Will Do** (DMTYSYWD – a much larger town, probably somewhere else) - that is even better. That is being proactive.

Doing more can be implemented in small ways:

- Delivering a product or service a little sooner than quoted
- For slightly less than the quoted price

Or we can create a much bigger impact, for example:

- Offering to loan a product for a few days rather than the usual 10-minute look in the showroom. I heard an example of a well-known department store delivering a fridge/freezer to a customer so that they could live with it for a few days. Needless to say, they bought it

Proactive Communication
This is huge and makes a massive difference to customer perception. Here are some ideas. See if you can come up with some of your own too.

- When we meet a customer, we can be proactive and initiate the conversation ourselves, rather than wait for them to start talking to us
- When a customer has a product or service ordered, we can make regular calls or send messages to keep them updated (rather than leaving them wondering) and perhaps check if we can be of further service
- When a customer asks for advice or information that we don't have to hand, we can offer to find it out and call the customer back (and then DWYSYWD)

- When it appears that a customer doesn't understand or is confused, we can acknowledge that and explore ways to help
- We can also offer tips and advice to help the customer get the most from using their new product or service (more about this in Part 3)

One of my favourite proactive communication techniques is **signposting**. This is when we explain in advance to a customer or client what will happen. An example of this is when we go down to breakfast in a hotel. When we arrive, they explain things like who will be looking after us today, where the self-service area is, what menu options need to be cooked to order, how long this will take, and so on. As a customer, it helps us to relax and to feel comfortable. As a service provider, it enables us to manage the customer's expectations and clear up any assumptions they may have.

The really important thing when signposting is to communicate the situation or process clearly to the customer in order for an agreement to be reached. For example, imagine that you are a website designer. You would want your customer to know that you have understood their brief and to check that your understanding is correct. More than that, you would want your customer to know the anticipated timescales and how the process works. At what stages will you be getting in touch with the customer for their approval of the design? How many design options will be offered? How many times are you willing to refine the design? What information and content will you require from them? By when? It's fantastic for ensuring that there are no assumptions that haven't been expressed, allowing us to reach an agreement before moving forward.

Let me finish this chapter with a story about a time when the staff of a hotel were extremely proactive in making me feel welcome and valued as a guest.

The hotel was in a lovely location with perfect views of the English countryside, but on entering the hotel I didn't receive a great first impression. The carpet was worn and as I looked more closely there were other signs that the hotel had seen better days. Yet, as I arrived in the bedroom I noticed that there was a small box on the bed containing four hand-made Belgian chocolates. Next to the chocolates was an envelope containing a card with a drawing of the hotel on the front. Inside, beautifully written with a fountain pen, were the following words: 'Dear Mr Collett, a very warm welcome to our hotel' and it was signed by the General Manager. Some years later, on a return visit, the welcome card read 'Dear Mr Collett, a very warm welcome back to our hotel' - acknowledging that I had stayed there before.

How much time do you think it takes a General Manager to write a personal welcome card for new guests each day? 30 minutes? My guess is that it's the most productive 30 minutes of their day. I've told this story many times. A great example of a team being proactive with their customers.

What extra special actions could you take to cherish your customers?

....
....
....
....
....
....
....
....
....

Action tips

- Proactively look for ways to be of service to customers
- Always be looking to create a 'wow', perhaps by doing some really simple, thoughtful act
- Use signposting as a way to manage our customers' expectations and reach clear agreements with them

7. BE A TEAM PLAYER

The customer experience is the result of how a team functions. It's always a team effort. Everyone involved plays their part, whether they are dealing directly with the end customer or providing support to those who are doing that. This is the concept of having internal customers who also deserve a HUG.

There's no greater test of a team's ability to function than when things don't go according to plan. When things go wrong, or if a customer isn't happy, everyone needs to make it their business to do whatever they can to correct the situation, irrespective of which department or individual it was that may have messed up.

If a customer came to you and gave a sincere compliment about their experience and it wasn't something that you personally did, the likelihood is that you would graciously accept the positive feedback, thank the customer and pass it on to the person concerned. You wouldn't say 'I don't work in that department'. That would totally throw the compliment back in the customer's face and you just wouldn't do it. So, when it's something less than positive, how about we adopt the same approach? What would that look and sound like?

The first thing is to apologise. Now, I'm aware that many people have a point of view about this - concerned that we might be admitting that we fell short, and maybe it wasn't even our fault. So, the apology doesn't need to be 'I'm sorry we messed up' or 'I'm sorry we got it wrong' – unless we clearly did. It can be more of an 'I'm sorry to hear that' type of apology. Do it sincerely, with the right energy, body language, facial expression and voice tone. (Don't be defensive!) Follow up the apology with 'Let me see what I can do to help'. People want to feel that they have been acknowledged and heard.

Be a Corsican

Find a way – not an excuse

Whether we are in a challenging situation or not, it's great to always be a Corsican. Someone with an attitude of 'course I can'. While we may not always immediately see a solution, we can tell ourselves 'there must be a way to solve this – I just haven't discovered it yet'. When we say this in our heads, it sets the unconscious mind to work on discovering a solution. However, when we say to ourselves 'there's no way to solve this' our mind won't even try and so it becomes a self-fulfilling prophesy, closing down possibilities rather than starting a mind-Google search for possible solutions.

By taking responsibility for the problem, we become a positive influence in our team. Even if we work in a really strongly bonded team, there's always scope for improvement. We can be a role-model for others and we may well find that the culture in the team shifts, for example:

- The team becomes one in which colleagues always support each other instead of blaming
- The team becomes one that focuses on success rather than on what is lacking

When things go well, be gracious and acknowledge that we didn't do it entirely alone. Even if we work out in the field making our own appointments and negotiating our own deals, the likelihood is that there were others involved, perhaps producing excellent point-of-sale materials, or even delivering the products or services themselves.

Share the love… Colleagues need a HUG too!

Talking of which, how does your team deal with negativity? How willing are you and your colleagues to deal with issues in order to keep the customer happy and coming back?

These are questions to recall when you reach Chapter 18 (Heal a Relationship)!

Action tips

- Take ownership whenever a problem arises, be a *Corsican!*
- Offering a sincere apology early in the conversation will help to defuse the customer's frustration
- Share successes with colleagues – spread the love!

---

8. UNDERSTAND NEEDS AND EXPECTATIONS

If we are going to be excellent at customer service, we need to understand what our customers' needs are and what they expect. Why is this important?

Customers contact us for a reason. Sometimes they find it difficult to articulate that reason. Sometimes they want to play a game of 'I'm not telling you' because they think we'll use the information against them (i.e. to sell them something they don't want). So when customers get in touch, they have needs (or if you prefer, requirements) and they would like some assistance to have them fulfilled.

The thing is, if we don't satisfy their needs, they won't buy from us. We will end up doing the familiar 'feature dump' reeling off all the different features of a whole list of products in the hope that something will click.

Take 1. Let's say a customer is going to buy a washing machine. They visit an electrical warehouse. The assistant asks 'Can I help you?' They respond with 'I'm interested in a washing machine'. The assistant says 'Great! Follow me…' and proceeds to begin a run-through of all the machines on offer explaining all the features whether they are relevant to the customer or not (probably reading the point-of-sale material, as if the customer was not able to read that for themselves). By the time they reach the end of the row, the customer has zoned out.

Take 2. Let's say the customer visits another electrical store where they say the same opening words. The assistant says 'OK, great. We have a big range of machines and I'm sure we'll find you the right one. **What are the most important features you are looking for in your next washing machine?'** *There's the magic.* The customer replies 'Well, it must have a 1400 spin speed, it's got to take a 10kg load and cost no more than £500'.

The assistant is then able to answer 'OK. Based on that, we have three machines to show you. Let me run through the pros and cons of each one'. Bingo! However, that's pretty rare in my experience.

Now let's take it to another level. When the assistant has established what the customer needs from their new washing machine, and before showing them the three machines that all fit the bill, here's another question they could ask: **'Why are those features in particular important to you?'** Wow! Have you ever been asked that in an electrical store? How might the customer answer? 'Well, we don't want to use a tumble dryer, we dry our clothes on a rail, so the drier the clothes come out of the machine the better. Also, we care for an elderly relative and we have to change the bedding quite frequently, so it's handy if all the bedding can go together in one load. And, we're working to a budget because we don't want to take out a loan.'

So, there we see the power of 'why' - we get to **understand their reasons**. We'll stand out head and shoulders from all our competitors. Our customers will love us. And on the way home from work, we'll be feeling great knowing that we have been of service and made a positive difference in the lives of others.

One word of caution. Be careful asking 'why' questions. If they are not asked in the right way it can seem like we are challenging the customer: 'Why do you want one of those?' 'Why do you need that?' The customer might then feel that they need to justify themselves.

We just need to ensure that we ask 'why' questions in a curious and gentle way. If necessary, we can change the question into 'What would be the reason for…?' which is less direct and may elicit a more open response.

Action tips

- Be curious about what the customer needs – what do they want the product or service to **do** for them? Gently explore the reasons why those requirements are important to them
- Use that information to provide a laser-guided explanation of how your product or service perfectly fulfils their needs
- Use proactive communication to avoid misunderstandings

9. MAKE IT FEEL NATURAL

Have you ever been into a shop, hotel, restaurant or car dealership and felt that people weren't really being genuine? (Perhaps they had just been on a customer service training course and were reciting a script!) How was that for you as a customer? For me, when this happens, I feel disappointed.

What would be your ideal? Welcoming, friendly and easy? I'm guessing that you have had some great experiences as a customer - times when you felt completely at ease and the whole experience just flowed.

A coffee shop I used to go to regularly (before I moved to another area) is great. I loved going there. I got to know the manager, Bam, he's a really cool dude. One of the things he loved about working there is the dress code. There isn't one! He went to work wearing clothes that express who he really is, as did all his team members. Sure, they all wore the company aprons, but beyond that, it seemed like anything goes! It was awesome. Everyone – customers and staff – seemed really relaxed! One of the main reasons that Bam loved working there was not the pay, the hours, the pension, or the annual leave. It was just the fact that he could be who he is. And, you know, when that's the deal for the staff, it's an invitation to the customers too. I would feel that I can be who I am, which is another thing I loved about going there – it felt great!

Let the Customer Meet the Real You

Even if the coffee shop vibe isn't the deal where you work, you can look for ways to let your true identity show. Customers are after connection. Being yourself is an invitation for the customer to be who they are. If you are relaxed, the customer will be too.

OK, maybe we're in a situation where we're required to say certain things, ask certain questions, or wear certain clothes.

Maybe it's company policy or a legal requirement. Fair enough. Follow protocol but go ahead and put some fun and personality around it.

Make It Your Own

Use a tone of voice that says we really 'own' what we're saying and doing. Include an extra bit of conversation. I have seen this done so well in many situations. When a person has a spark about them it completely changes the interaction. We absolutely don't need to sound bored.

I mentioned the 'Pike Place Fish Video' earlier, and it's a great source of ideas for how to go about this. One technique they have perfected is when a member of their team calls out an order, the whole team chants it right back at them. That's just one creative suggestion for transforming a repetitive daily routine into something that customers can tell their families about. The employees aren't reciting a script they are being themselves and having fun.

Much more on this in Part 3, but in the meantime, ask yourself 'How could I be myself and have more fun at work?'

....
....
....
....

Action tips

- Find creative ways to have fun at work
- Let your personality shine through your words and actions
- Get your team involved – spread the magic

10. DO MORE THAN EXPECTED

Most of us like to feel that we have come out on top in some way.
Personally, I love a bargain and there doesn't need to be a massive saving for it to feel good, although the bigger the better! Even a small saving or a freebie does the trick.

I recently had a meal in a Thai restaurant with a friend and we both ordered a glass of the same wine. The waiter returned and, after he had poured the wine, he noticed that there was a small amount of the wine left in the bottle. With no hesitation, he said 'Here you go, I'll leave you what's left in the bottle'. There wasn't even that much wine left but it was a nice gesture; a small touch that made us feel valued.

Even though we often know that the cost of a 'free' item is hidden in the overall price, it feels as if we are getting it for nothing. Many of us love all-inclusive holidays because, for the time that we are away, we're not spending money. It feels as if it's free even though we pre-paid for our food and drinks. Perception is everything.

Add Value
I always look for ways to do this with my clients. I'll agree on a fee, knowing that I'm going to give them more than they think they are getting. Sometimes it's a gift of a book or another type of added value such as additional follow-up support. Plus I'll often send a 'thank you' card to express my appreciation for their business. Psychologically this works really well. It's an investment in the relationship, communicates caring, and says 'this is not just about the money'.

What about for you? What could you do? Maybe a little free gift – some small, thoughtful touch. The more relevant to the customer we can make it, the better. Maybe we can add value and be of service in other ways: offer some tips on how to use the product, a money-off voucher for next time, or give them access to a VIP members group. It doesn't need to be costly; it just needs a bit of creative thought, planning and time. If you can't give a physical gift, offer an emotional one – kind words, appreciation or a hug.

Make our customer's day by doing something extra special.

What could you do?

....
....
....
....
....
....
....
....
....
....

And when things go wrong, see it as an opportunity. Research has shown that when a problem arises, if the situation is handled well customers can become *more* loyal than they were before! (By the way, this is not a suggestion to create problems for your customers!)

So, when things go wrong, don't just put the situation right. We could just correct the mistake and leave it at that - believing that we have done what we needed to do - but remember, we also need to repair the damage that has been done to both the relationship and our reputation in the customer's mind. Do something to say 'sorry'. Give a gift of some kind. Leave them feeling that the problem wasn't so bad after all.

When I ran a car dealership, if a customer had a problem with their car, we would lend them a courtesy car – whenever possible, a better model than their own car, perhaps a nice convertible. The customer might say to themselves 'This is a very nice car to drive around in. I don't mind how long it takes the dealer to fix my car!' Sometimes we would even say to the customer 'Thank you for your patience. Please take your partner out to dinner and bring us the bill'. It works.

What could you do in your situation?

....
....
....
....
....
....
....
....
....
....
....

Action tips

- Look for ways to show customers that you appreciate and value them
- When making commitments to customers, build-in some 'going beyond' room – around price, timescale, service level, etc.
- See 'problems' as 'opportunities' – to wow the customer and leave them feeling better than before

PLUS ONE – COMMIT TO YOUR OWN DEVELOPMENT

It's not about being the best

It's about being better than you were yesterday

In the spirit of Chapter 10 - Do More Than Expected - here's a bonus chapter!

Do you know any 'junkies'? I'm not talking about people addicted to illegal substances, but I am talking about people who are always reading self-development books and going on courses and retreats.

Well, I am one of those people. I have spent thousands of pounds (I haven't dared to do the maths) on personal development materials.

Speaking from experience, it can all become a bit of a fixation and you know what? I thoroughly recommend it. Surprisingly, life on a development path doesn't always get easier (although it can). What I have found though, is that it does get a whole lot more exciting in so very many ways.

Below are a few suggestions for self-development that will sky-rocket your career. It doesn't need to cost you anything because there's loads of great information available for free on the internet, including at servicewithahug.com

NLP – Neuro Linguistic Programming
As was mentioned earlier, NLP offers a number of tools and techniques that help us to communicate more effectively. NLP

helps us to manage our response to any situation that may crop up, allowing us to stay resourceful and achieve the results we desire.

For more information search for NLP online.

Emotional Intelligence

EI was brought to prominence by Daniel Goleman in the 1970s. Daniel found that academic ability and IQ are not the predictors of success that we might expect them to be. We've all come across stories of people who were really intellectual but haven't been successful. Similarly, we've heard about those who had little or no educational qualifications but are very successful at creating the lifestyle they want. Good examples of this are Richard Branson and Sir Alan Sugar.

So, what does it boil down to? The ability to manage ourselves and create effective relationships with others. Particularly our ability to influence, persuade and inspire people.

For more information search for Emotional Intelligence online.

Self-Awareness

How self-aware are you? What is self-awareness anyway?

Personally, I would define self-awareness as an understanding of how we operate in the world – our beliefs, our values, our behaviour and so on. In addition to that, it's appreciating our impact on others and how they perceive us.

This is very useful information. At the same time, it's something you may not have given this much thought to.

Let's consider the following:

- Looking at your early life story, which people, events, and experiences have had the greatest impact in shaping the person you have become?
- How do others perceive you?
- How well do you know yourself?
- What are your strengths?
- What are your weaknesses?
- How do you prefer to do things?

There are very many different ways to be a human being. None of them are 'right' or 'wrong'. But that's not the point. Other people will always have thoughts about the way we do things and may make us 'wrong' in their minds. Raising our awareness of the impact we have on others means that we can change our behaviour to accommodate different circumstances, particularly in customer service situations where the aim is to achieve a happy customer. I would encourage you to seek honest feedback from others – customers, colleagues, friends, family members and so on. One note of caution: make it easy for people to speak honestly – you don't want them saying what they think you want to hear. Invite constructive suggestions and thank them sincerely. Avoid offering them your point of view as this may seem like you are being defensive and may put people off giving you feedback in the future. How they see it is how they see it. End of.

For more information search for Self Awareness online.

Mindfulness

When is the last time you took the time to do nothing? To take time out for yourself? It can be incredibly beneficial, both mentally and physically, to meditate regularly. People who meditate talk about greater calmness and mental focus. I wonder what it could be for you...

For more information search for Mindfulness online.

Action tips

- Consider some ways in which you could develop your skills. Do a bit of research and then make a commitment to one thing – a book, a course, a webinar – just take the next step and see where it leads
- Ask others how they see you – your regular customers, trusted colleagues, friends, relatives – use their feedback as a valuable resource for your future development
- Learn to meditate and commit to a daily mindfulness practice – even if it's just 10 minutes in the morning before you start your day

---

PART 2
UNDERSTAND EMOTIONALLY

Always render more and better service than is expected of you, no matter what your task may be

Og Mandino

Welcome to the second part of our book. In Part 1 we explored ways to - 'H' - handle our customers skilfully. In theory, if you did only that and nothing else you'd be *way* ahead of the game based on my experiences of being a customer. I've worked in customer service roles for my entire working life, including training customer-facing staff for over two decades. One thing I've noticed is the high degree of attention that gets paid to *what* to say and do rather *how* to *be* with customers.

You'll notice that Part 1 was primarily about *what* to do. Let's now explore *how* we are *being*. What are we bringing to each interaction with customers and colleagues? What is our intention? What is our *energy*?

Here in Part 2 – 'U' – we will explore ways to understand our customers and colleagues emotionally (which will also require an understanding of our own emotional states), and about the difference 'U' can make. It is perhaps the most important area of all three aspects of HUG.

Why is understanding our customer's emotional state so important, or even relevant? Because most customers don't decide who to buy from based on logic - there's a good deal of emotion in there. Most of us buy from people we like and trust - a level of connection we need to encourage with all our customers, but to do that we need to understand the impact we are making on our customers and an understanding of how to lead customers into a more positive frame of mind when being of service to them.

So, let's get going....

11. RECOGNISING THE SIGNS

Think about a time when, as a customer yourself, you experienced the service provider being distracted, perhaps even having a conversation with a colleague, or simply just being disengaged. You probably felt something – perhaps irritated, frustrated or annoyed – feelings that will have been obvious to anyone else observing the situation. But the service provider, off in their own world, was probably unaware of those signals from you. When have we been unaware of our impact with our own customers?

Each customer is constantly giving us lots of information about how they are feeling, even if they are not interacting verbally with us. They are giving off an energy. Everyone does it, whether they are aware of it or not. More about this later in the book... keep reading!

If you are physically with the customer, watch their body language closely for signs.

- They may be feeling a little anxious or nervous, a feeling that can be brought on by being out of their comfort zone or the fear of making a wrong decision
- Alternatively, they may be feeling very excited because today is the day they are going to get their long wished for product and they can't wait

What differences would you notice in the body language of the two customers in the examples above? The likelihood is that you don't actually need to be told – intuitively, you know already. It's instinctive. As mentioned in Part 1, it's that primitive part of us that was hardwired to assess a situation. We all know how to do this even if we might be a bit rusty. I'd sum this up as 'listening to your intuition', which some people call 'gut feel'.

What else can we pick up on? How about tone of voice? This is particularly important when we are dealing with customers on the telephone and we don't have body language to offer further information. See Chapter 15 for more on this.

Pay attention!
When we pay attention, *really* pay attention, something magical happens. Listening for the emotion behind the words, watching the body language for small clues and connecting with what they might be feeling helps us to see the world through their eyes. When we put ourselves in the customer's shoes we are able to align with their needs and respond accordingly.
I'd like to recommend a book for further examples of what is possible. 'Time to Think' by Nancy Kline invites us to develop the art of paying full attention to what the other person is saying, and not just in words. In her book, Nancy presents a step-by-step guide that can be used in any situation. Whether we want to have more productive meetings, solve business problems or build stronger relationships, this book offers a new world of possibilities.

Distractions
With so many distractions these days, it's quite usual to be partially focused on our devices rather than giving full attention to the other person or people in the conversation. It has almost become the norm to have mobiles flashing updates from social media sites whilst in the middle of a conversation. Are we really so indispensable that we can't put our phone away for the duration of the conversation? Or is this merely a habit? If it's the latter, you'll know that habits can change – just ask an ex-smoker. And changing this could be equally as impactful as giving up smoking.

Giving someone the gift of our attention is one of the most powerful ways of 'wowing' our customer, simply because it's pretty unusual. When you do so, you'll be much more tuned in to the customer. You'll have a deeper connection with them and a far better sense of how to create that memorable customer experience.

Action tips

- Be very aware of your customer's body language and voice tone
- Avoid distractions and give the customer the gift of your full attention
- Trust your knowing – your 'gut'

---

12. MATCH

What is your understanding of the word rapport? In Chapter 2 (Connect) we described it as a 'personal connection with warmth'. The Oxford English Dictionary offers us: 'A close and harmonious relationship in which the people or groups concerned understand each other's feelings or ideas and communicate well'.

My take on rapport is that it's a feeling. When we have rapport, it feels comfortable, easy and there's warmth on both sides. We can relax and be ourselves. Without rapport, an exchange is transactional and cold and we might feel a bit on edge. Another way to describe it might be connected vs. disconnected.

In a customer service context, we don't really want 'close relationships' – imagine how busy we would be on social media - but we do want rapport. An exception might involve selling something of very high value with an extended sales process and where we have relatively few customers.

And why might rapport be important? Hopefully it's obvious. Customers enjoy that feeling of ease, of being connected. This links massively to trust. When there's rapport, there's generally trust. Without rapport, there's usually less trust which prompts a guarded, arm's length way of doing business.

Rapport is a huge driving force in keeping customers coming back. How many of your customers just randomly contact you or drop by, not because they need to purchase anything, but because they just feel like keeping in touch? Those are the customers with whom you have great rapport and the chances are they love doing business with you.

One of the easiest ways to build rapport is to just be curious about the other person; show a keen interest in their favourite subject which is... themselves! Dale Carnegie wrote the book 'How to Win Friends and Influence People' in 1936 and it continues to be a life-changing book for those who read it. When I read the book I discovered that people are 100 times more interested in themselves than they are in you. It's so clear! Encourage people to talk about themselves and they'll love you!

Which brings us to Matching - the title of this chapter. What's the link between rapport and matching? Well, at the heart of rapport is *similarity*. We feel a sense of ease with people with whom we have a shared way of experiencing the world and something in common. You like fishing, they like fishing. Hurrah, let's talk about maggots! Just kidding, but you get the point. It really is that easy.

But here's the key question: can we build rapport with someone with whom we have no shared interest? What do you think? Have a look back at what you wrote down in response to those questions in Chapter 2 (Connect).
I'm guessing that a great many of the connections you have are based around a shared interest – football, fishing, yoga, drama, music. You feel on the same wavelength as the other person, and therefore it's easy to connect.

This won't always be the case with your customers. So how do you create a feeling of 'we're on the same wavelength' with someone who may not have the same interests as you? Well, the clue is in the title of this chapter. We match them. We do our own version of them. Not in a mimicking way. Not in a manipulative way. But in a way that says 'I'd really like to create some warmth and connection in this interaction'.

So, what can be matched? The most powerful rapport-builders are those aspects that the other person isn't even aware of. Let's look at a few now.

Body Language

As a service provider, when we notice aspects of the customer's body language, it puts us in the driving seat in terms of how connected we feel to that person. If they have a particular way of sitting or standing (and we all do), we can adopt a similar posture. If they like to use certain gestures, we can use them too. You might think that this is really obvious and the other person will notice it straight away. In my experience, that's not the case. But they definitely will *feel* the effect. They will begin to relax and feel more comfortable and yet they won't really know why. But you will.

Voice

Pay attention to how the other person speaks. Do they speak quickly or slowly? Do they pause or not? Do they use a lot of energy in their voice or not so much? However they like to speak, you can do your version of it (subtly, without overtly imitating them).
Is this sounding like fun?

Words

Most people have favourite words - words that crop up again and again in their speech. Listen for those words and use them. Here's an example in which the service provider is matching the customer's words:

> *Customer:* Hi! I'm looking for a new TV. 4K with amazing styling and a wall bracket so as I can watch it from wherever I am in the room. I've looked all over town but can't see one that I like the look of... You got anything here?

> *Service Provider:* Hi! Well, thanks for coming in to see us today! Seems to me you've got a really clear vision of what you want. I get the picture and I'll be happy to show you our range. Let me check first that I've got

clarity. It appears to me that you want a 4K TV with amazing styling and a wall bracket so you can watch from wherever you are in the room.

Customer: Bullseye!

Service Provider: Great, that's clear. Before I show you, are there any other features you're looking for? We don't want to miss anything...

What do you notice about what the service provider is saying in this interaction? What do you notice about their communication style and choice of words?

....
....
....
....
....
....
....
....
....

In this example, the customer is likely to feel they've found someone just like them. They may not think it consciously and that's the beauty of using this technique. It's very subtle and incredibly powerful, but mastering it needs practice.

So, what was the service provider doing? They were using the customer's exact words back to them and adding their own words in a similar style. If you really study the language, you'll see that most of the customer's words are 'visual' – looking for... styling... looked all over town... can't see one I like the look of... Notice that the service provider matches that communication style - coming in to see us... I get the picture... show you... got clarity... it appears to me... that's clear... before I show you... anything else you're looking for?

My experience of using a technique like this is that the customer feels magnetically drawn to us - as if by magic! They feel as if we 'get them' which, of course, we do!

Not every customer will prefer visual language. Some will tend to use sound based (known as 'auditory') words like 'I hear you', 'that rings a bell', 'sounds good', 'give me a shout', 'on my wavelength', 'living in harmony', 'music to my ears', etc. Some will prefer feelings-based (known as 'kinaesthetic') words like 'get a grip', 'keep in touch', 'feels right', 'roughly the same', 'things went smoothly', etc.

Imagine using auditory or kinaesthetic language with our example above when the customer was using visual words. They would more than likely have walked out thinking that the service provider didn't understand what they were 'looking' for!

There's one other thing to point out in the example above - the service provider matched the customer's level of formality. Notice the greeting – the customer leads with 'Hi!' so the service provider mirrors that. Imagine how the customer would have felt if the response had come back formally with 'Good morning, Sir'. The service provider would have immediately put distance between him/herself and the customer. While we always need to keep in mind that we are representing a business or organisation (so therefore we need to remain professional), it is possible to flex within a range.

I encourage you to play with this and notice the results you get. Have fun with it – you may be better at it than you think!

Action tips

- Adopt your own version of the customer's body language
- Match the tempo, tonality and energy of the customer's voice
- Pay attention to the customer's language (visual, auditory or kinaesthetic) and adopt similar language yourself

13. EMPATHISE

What is empathy? Some would say it is 'Acknowledging the feelings of the other person'. Many customer service books and training courses will emphasise the need for empathy when things go wrong and the customer is upset. It's true; empathy is a vital ingredient in these situations. I would suggest going further. How about using it all the time?

Why empathise with people? What does it create? First and foremost, it creates more ease between us and them. Building on Chapter 12 about Matching, empathy adds to our sense of understanding, similarity and connection. When someone empathises with us, we feel understood, and also feel that our emotions have been acknowledged. And as with rapport, there is a link between empathy and trust. The two seem to go hand in hand. And it's clear to see why this would be a good thing – customers who trust us buy from us. And if they trust our advice, they will come back again and again. Our advice is one of the ways we can add value. More about this in Part 3.

What about the customer? What does more trust do for them? Some say that it is one of the most important elements for a customer. When customers feel genuine empathy and begin to trust, it puts the customer's mind at ease.

Everyone, not just our customers, will love that feeling. This definitely applies to colleagues too. What if we notice that someone at work doesn't seem their usual selves? Can we offer some empathy and emotional support in that situation? Of course! Check in with them. Have a coffee together. Invite them to open up. There's much more awareness of mental health and wellbeing these days. It's OK to not feel OK. It really helps to talk. You can be the one who offers some empathy and understanding. Use the guidelines below.

There are many ways to express empathy.

- **Allow space –** give the other person space to speak. Some of us may have felt uncomfortable with silence. And yet, it's sometimes what is needed. Be sure to allow enough space for the other person to finish speaking. Avoid jumping in straight away or, even worse, talking over the other person

- **Warm words** – phrases such as 'I understand...' and 'I appreciate...' will build a sense of empathy and emotional connection. As will asking questions such as 'How do you feel about that?' which show that we are interested in the other person's feelings

- **Gentle eye Contact** – one of the primary ways of making a connection with someone else is through the eyes. We often show our emotions through our eyes (anger or sadness for example) so it's important that we maintain soft, caring eye contact. See Chapter 16 for more on eye contact

- **Active Listening** – what do we mean by 'active' listening? What is the difference between 'listening' and 'active listening'? The active part is the feedback which lets others know we are listening. Feedback involves **eye contact** as well as **nodding in acknowledgement** and a **verbal response**.

- **Body Language** – remain open, relaxed and supple as signs of tension can be picked up by the other person outside of their conscious awareness which in turn affects their level of ease. Avoid gestures or postures that could be interpreted by the other as 'closed' or 'defensive'. Try gently 'leaning in' to them whilst respecting their personal space. Another important element of body language is our facial expression. Maintain a warm, neutral facial expression with a genuine smile

---

Action tips

- Remember to sense how others might be feeling and to acknowledge that if appropriate – trust your knowing
- Adjust your body language to help the customer or colleague feel more comfortable
- Use supportive, encouraging words and phrases

---

14. HAVE FUN

*People will forget what you said, people will forget
what you did, but people will never forget how you
made them feel*

Maya Angelou

As a customer, I often wonder how much fun the person I'm
dealing with is having. Sometimes I'm not wondering for long –
it becomes obvious really quickly, and not always in a good
way.

A customer usually has a great experience when dealing with a
service provider who has a positive attitude, or mindset. Some
people go the extra mile for their customers, making their day
through a bright and cheerful approach. Some people show up,
do their job and go home. The former says 'I'm here for you,
how can I serve you, how can I add some value and cheer you
up?' The latter could be interpreted as 'I don't care'.

It's essential that we make the customer experience
memorable and fun if we would like customers to come back.

How much fun do you have at work? What would happen if you
started having more fun? Even just a tiny one percent? My bet
is that at least three things would happen. Firstly, your
customers would be uplifted by their interaction with you.
Secondly, you would enjoy your day more. Thirdly, your
colleagues would also enjoy the experience. To me, this is a no-
brainer!

What stops us having fun at work? Sometimes the answer to
that is 'nothing'. So, what are we waiting for? It won't happen by
itself; we need to create it.

I would encourage you to regularly have fun at work. Build it into your day. Make it part of the team culture where you work. You'll find that having fun is contagious; it will spread like wildfire, and the energy level will rise accordingly.

'But you don't know what it's like where I work, it's impossible to have fun' I hear you say. It could be true that your employer expects you to deal with customers in a particular way and you must keep your behaviour appropriate for the brand or industry you represent. At the same time, you can find opportunities to keep things light and help the day go along nicely.

I once met someone who worked for an undertaker. He explained that while dealing with grieving relatives it is, of course, completely inappropriate to be jolly, laughing and making jokes. Yet behind the scenes, it was quite normal for them to have fun while carrying out their unusual work!

Creating a fun atmosphere at work (without going over the top) will lift the atmosphere and make everyone feel better. As I said before, always making sure that if there are customers around you include them so that they don't think that you're having a laugh at their expense.

So, go ahead, make someone's day... and your own...

Action tips

- Actively look for opportunities to keep your working environment light and playful, whilst remaining appropriate to the industry you work in
- Make your customer's day by creating a relaxed, memorable and fun experience each time
- Put up a visual reminder of Maya Angelou's quote

15. TONE OF VOICE

'It's not what you say, it's how you say it'.

The real meaning of what is being said is carried by the tone of voice. It's all about the energy!

When I was managing a sales team, one of my salespeople was able to say the most outrageous things to his customers yet they loved it and they loved him. He loved his work, he loved making his customers laugh and that is what came through in his tone of voice. He was being totally authentic, being his own amusing self and not just following a sales script. That's what customers want – authentic connection in every area of their life, even in momentary, everyday interactions.

Try this easy little experiment. Say this phrase and emphasise the word in italics. See how it changes the meaning. Try it with someone else and get them to say what meaning they hear each time.

What was said	(What was communicated)
I didn't say she stole your purse...	(someone else said it)
I **didn't** say she stole your purse...	(I said something else)
I didn't **say** she stole your purse...	(I might have implied it)
I didn't say **she** stole your purse...	(someone else did it)
I didn't say she **stole** your purse...	(she did something else with it)
I didn't say she stole **your** purse...	(she stole someone else's purse)
I didn't say she stole your **purse**...	(she stole something else)

The same sentence communicating seven very different messages. Equally, 'Have a nice day' can easily come across as 'I really don't want to be here doing this boring job' - if that's what we're thinking and feeling. Customers not only sense that it's fake but they 'get' the real meaning by our tone of voice. They sense our energy.

So, the big question is how do we actually set the *tone* for our interactions?

You recall from earlier in the book how essential it is to make **a positive first impression**. We need to set the tone for our interaction with the customer – perhaps something playful, caring, upbeat, and confident. As you now know, once we have made our first impression it takes an overwhelming amount of effort to make the customer admit to themselves that they were 'wrong' about us at first. We decide something about someone and then all we want to do is be right – that's human nature. We unconsciously look for facts and evidence to support our point of view and dismiss anything that doesn't fit. This applies to customers, colleagues and of course us.

Let's look at how we might play around with different voice tones. Try saying the same thing whilst applying a selection of tones. Find someone who can play this game with you and get them to describe what they hear in your voice.
Try saying something like 'The café is located on the third floor' as if you are:

- Irritated
- Interested
- Bored
- Caring
- Stern
- Patronising
- Angry

Think about the impact we make when speaking on the telephone. It's said that 82% of impact will be made from tone of voice with only 18% from the words spoken. Plus there are added dimensions to telephone communication:

- The telephone has a tendency to make the voice sound a little flat. So it's a good idea to raise our energy level to beyond how it would be if we were speaking to someone face-to-face. If we don't do this, we can sound as if we've had an enthusiasm bypass! I recently called an up-market department store in London for the first time. The recorded welcome message was dull and flat. It totally lacked energy, excitement or passion which created a really poor first impression

- Another factor to take into account is that we cannot be sure what's going on at the other end, what activity they might be involved in. We can't see them and they can't see us. This applies to the customer too. Let them know what you're doing, for example, "I'm just calling that information up on my screen right now Mr. Customer. It's just taking a moment... (If there's a wait) How's your day going so far?"

- Another thing we can do is convey a positive emotion by smiling – yes it really is possible to hear a smile at the other end of the telephone! Try it out for yourself

- Generally, we are unaware of how we sound to others on the telephone. We can learn a great deal about our impact by recording calls and listening back to how we sound

Ask a few other people whom you trust to comment on how you sound on the phone and ask for suggestions. They may come up with things like:

- Slow down
- Create more of a connection with the customer
- Inject more energy and passion
- Allow more time for the customer to finish speaking
- Breathe and speak more from the belly than from the throat (this results in the voice resonating at a lower frequency and therefore conveying more credibility and authority)

In summary, our tone of voice reveals a great deal about how we are experiencing our world, which in turn has an impact on our customers. If we are in a negative state we can change how we feel by:

- Having some friendly banter with a colleague
- Taking a break and getting some fresh air
- Taking deep, relaxing breaths
- Listening to some uplifting music
- Playing a game

I used to play an entertaining game with colleagues where we would give each other a random word (e.g. 'Walrus', 'Degenerate', 'Hopscotch', 'Electron' etc.) Our challenge was to then use that word in the next 10 customer interactions. Telling the customer about the game was considered cheating. Simple yet hilarious! Please be careful when playing this game – always remain professional and respectful – giving the customer a great experience is always the priority.

Action tips

- Be sure of your intention when you speak – the true meaning will be conveyed in your voice tone
- Inject a bit more energy and sparkle into your voice when using the telephone – stand up if necessary
- Get some feedback about your voice tone and apply any suggestions that turn up consistently

16. EYE CONTACT

As was mentioned earlier in the book, with great eye contact we come across as more engaged, friendly, and confident. Not only that, it provides us with a lot of non-verbal information about how the other person is feeling.

What stories do we make up about people when they aren't giving us much eye contact?

- They are shy
- They aren't telling the truth
- They lack confidence
- They are feeling anxious
- They aren't listening
- They aren't interested in us

Any of these could well be true - or none of them. They are just assumptions. You may also be aware that different cultures have different conventions regarding eye contact.

We can't control how much eye contact the customer is making with us. However, we can control our own eye contact and therefore avoid the customer making up a story about us. Eye contact is massive in terms of the impact it has on others. It's sometimes said that the eyes are the 'Window to the Soul'. Wow – what a thought! Imagine if we could connect with our customer's soul... (assuming they have one!). When someone looks into our eyes, at least there is something going on, some level of connection.

Of course, there are different qualities of eye contact. Too much intensity can feel uncomfortable - it can feel challenging or even threatening. The ideal is a soft, gentle eye contact, with our eyes meeting about 65-70% of the time - breaking eye contact every three to six seconds, and rather than looking down - which may indicate a lack of interest - look up or to the side as if you are thinking about what they are saying.

And rather than a 'manic stare' into the eyes, imagine an inverted triangle with a line across down to the tip of their nose. Placing our gaze into this 'eyes-nose' triangle gives the other person the feeling of eye contact, without the intensity of the manic stare. Try it. It's easy and it works.

Why should we care about this? Well, according to a British Psychological Society article from November 2016, 'we are more likely to **remember** faces with which we've experienced mutual gaze'. From a customer's perspective how great to be remembered from a previous visit and from a service provider's perspective, how great to have the customer remember us from last time! Not only that, we are also much more likely to trust each other and feel that we somehow care about each other.

So, how about setting an intention to improve eye contact? Here are a few suggestions to get started.

- Shorter conversations are easier than longer ones for maintaining eye contact, so start with quick, easy interactions and work up from there

- It's much easier to maintain eye contact when we are listening to someone than when we are speaking, so improve your 'listening' eye contact first and then move onto improving your 'speaking' eye contact

- Improve your eye contact with people you are comfortable with (friends, relatives, etc.) first, and when your confidence grows, develop stronger eye contact with people you find a bit intimidating (a boss, professional people, etc.)

Be kind to yourself and allow a bit of time for this new habit to feel natural.

Action tips

- Use eye contact as one way to connect with others and build trust
- Use the 'eyes-nose' triangle as a way to make eye contact more comfortable
- Start with easier conversations – then stretch yourself further

---

17. RELAX

It's all very well talking about getting our customers to feel like they've been hugged by us, but what if we're the ones who need the hug? What if we're feeling stressed and not in a good place emotionally with nothing left to give? Our customers will certainly pick up on how we're feeling, so we need to know how to care for ourselves emotionally. If we don't, we may experience physical, mental or emotional ill-health.

Most people go through times of feeling stressed at some point in their life. In fact, according to UK Government Statistics, 11.7 million working days were lost due to stress-related conditions in 2015/16 which was around 45% of all days lost to sickness. That's a lot!

Working in any role that involves dealing with customers has the potential to be stressful. What if the stress is not in the external event? What if it's our response to the event that creates a feeling of being stressed? I've noticed that two people can have a totally different response to the same event. For example, let's imagine you have been asked to give a talk about your role to thirty senior managers where you work. One person's response might be 'Great! I can't wait to do that. This is my opportunity to get noticed. I'm so excited!' Another person's response could be 'I'm terrified. I know I'll forget what to say and I'll look like an idiot. I'd rather do something else – anything else! My hands are going clammy now just thinking about it...'

Managing our stress can be made easier just by realising

that it's not about the external event, it's the story we made up in our heads that is causing the anxiety. 'It's an opportunity to get noticed' is one story and 'I know I'll forget what to say and I'll look like an idiot' is another. One of these might be true - or not.

'Whether we think we can - or whether we think we can't – either way, we're right!' - Henry Ford. It's a quote I love. Remember, our patterns of thought and unhelpful inner dialogue are the cause of our anxiety, not the event itself.

It's the story we tell ourselves that creates the experience. Therefore, when we gently question the story, the story can begin to change. Byron Katie uses the question 'Is that true?' in her approach called 'The Work'. For more information visit www.thework.com

We all maintain our wellbeing in different ways. The important thing is to know what works for us and then set aside the time to bring ourselves back into balance – ideally for a few minutes every day.

- For some people, exercise is a really effective way to release any tension in the body and therefore in the mind
- For others, something that involves relaxing the mind is preferable –meditation, mindfulness, listening to music with eyes closed, or reading a book
- Perhaps you like to feel nurtured, so a deep, hot, foamy bath is emotionally restorative, as are saunas, massage or other treatments for the body

- It's possible to combine both physical and mental aspects with practices like Yoga, Tai Chi, Qigong and other martial arts
- Slow, deep breathing is an amazing gateway into feeling more calm. Next time you feel some form of anxiety, stop and take a few breaths right into your belly and notice the difference it makes

If you are feeling stressed, talk to someone about it, don't pretend. The people around us can usually tell. There's no way to create an amazing experience for the customer if we're running on empty. We need to be at our best.

In summary, as they say in the aircraft safety briefing, put your own oxygen mask on first before helping others. Take care of yourself first – then you'll be in a position to take care of your customers.

Action tips

- Choose a way of relaxing that works for you – and make this a priority in your life
- When feelings of stress come up, remind yourself that it's the meaning we give a situation that causes the stressful reaction
- Take care of yourself first – the people in your life will thank you for that

18. HEAL A RELATIONSHIP

A traveller came upon an old farmer working in his field beside the road. Eager to rest his feet, the wanderer hailed the countryman, who seemed happy enough to straighten his back and pass the time of day.

"What sort of people live in the next town?" asked the stranger.

"What were the people like where you've come from?" replied the farmer, answering the question with another question.

"They were a bad lot. Troublemakers all, and lazy too. The most selfish people in the world, and not one of them to be trusted. I'm happy to be leaving the scoundrels."

"Is that so?" replied the old farmer. "Well, I'm afraid that you'll find the same sort in the next town.

Disappointed, the traveller trudged on his way, and the farmer returned to his work.

Some time later another stranger, coming from the same direction, hailed the farmer, and they stopped to talk. "What sort of people live in the next town?" he asked.

"What were the people like where you've come from?" replied the farmer once again.

"They were the best people in the world. Hard working, honest, and friendly. I'm sorry to be leaving them."

"Fear not," said the farmer. "You'll find the same sort in the next town."

Origin unknown

Do you have repeat customers? If not, you'll almost certainly have repeat *internal* customers – those all-important working relationships with colleagues. It makes no difference which it is for you. In either case, you're probably delighted to see some of them while, with others, maybe you can't wait for the conversation to end. Have you ever wondered why that is?

It's easier for us to make the other person responsible for the way the relationship works e.g. we may say 'She's so lovely, really easy to deal with' or 'He's a nightmare – nothing is ever good enough for him' and so on. Yet making the other person responsible means we are giving away our power and it can sometimes feel like we don't have a choice. The truth is we do. It takes two people to have a relationship and both will contribute positively or negatively to it. It's a dance. One person says or does something, and the other responds. Sometimes one person is leading and sometimes it's the other person's turn. Things are either getting better or worse. Factors that affect how things are between us and the customer can include:

- The first impression we made and how we set the tone for the conversation – Chapter 1 (Acknowledge) & Chapter 2 (Connect)
- The level of rapport between us and the customer – Chapter 2 (Connect) and Chapter 12 (Match)
- Previous interactions we may have had with this person (relationship history)
- Previous interaction/s the customer has had with someone else from our business (good, bad or mediocre) – Chapter 13 (Empathise)
- Our company's reputation – this is outside our direct control but by applying the principles in this book, we can positively influence it

- Things going on in our life outside of the interaction e.g. health issues, family/relationship challenges, money worries
- Things going on in the customer's life outside of the interaction e.g. health issues, family/relationship challenges, money worries

OK, so we know that we all have 'stuff' happening in our lives – emotional stuff. This applies to our customers and colleagues as much as ourselves. We know that these events can have a big impact on us. The next time you interact with someone and they are grumpy, lacking in patience or a bit short with you, I encourage you to forgive them. Who knows what is going on in their life? By the way, I'm not suggesting that you ask them. Just cut them some slack. Apply some empathy (Chapter 13). We don't know what the circumstances are and we don't know how we would be feeling if we were in the same situation.

It's easy to write them off as a 'miserable person' but, remember, we are never seeing the whole picture; just a very narrow slice.

If a customer is complaining about something that has gone wrong with the product or service our company supplied and their anger or frustration seems disproportionate, we can choose to just accept that it is what's happening and it isn't personal. Can you have no reaction? We can't possibly know how 'on the edge' they might be feeling emotionally. Often, the only thing people want is to be heard.

OK, so some customers and colleagues may have a track record of being difficult to deal with. Sometimes we get into a bit of a pattern. We have experienced them before and it wasn't pretty last time. They have experienced us before and they feel the same way. We, and the customer, have a particular mindset which creates an expectation which creates the experience. Let me explain using diagrams.

Firstly, here's how the fundamental principle works:

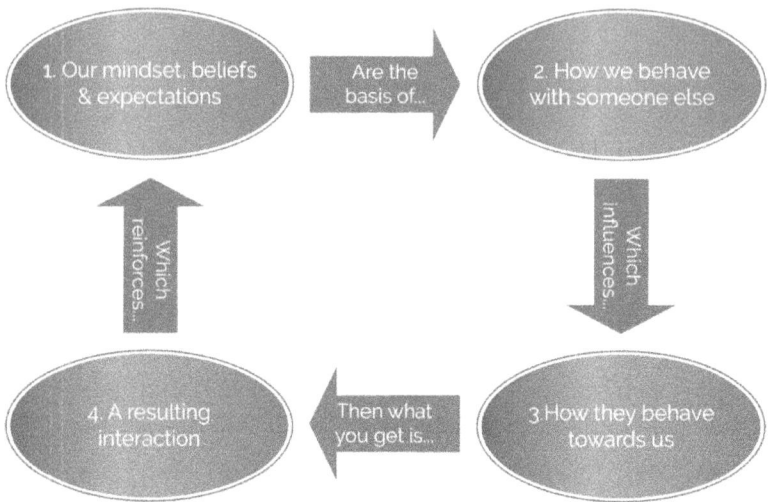

Now here's an example of how this might work with a 'difficult' customer:

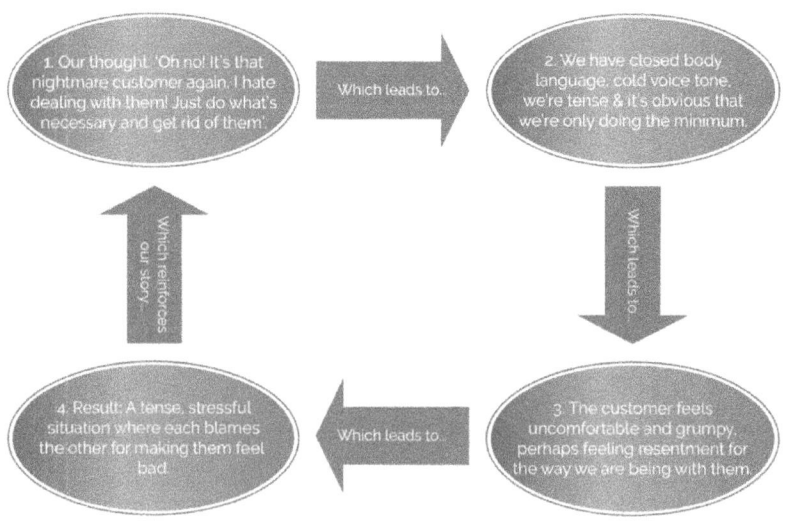

By way of contrast, here's an example of the principle in action with an 'easy' customer:

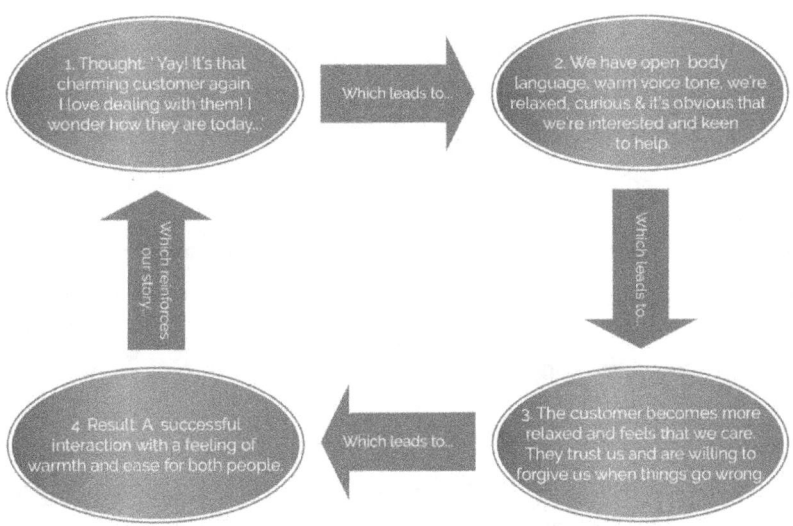

Here's a question for you: Do you have any customers or colleagues who were once 'difficult' who are now 'easy'?

When running workshops, I have never received a 'no' response to that question. Think about it for a moment. What happened to bring about the change? What did you do to create it? Did the other person just suddenly change? Or did you choose to see the situation and the person differently? Jot down what you remember:

....

....

....

....

....

....

....

Surely we would like to have better relationships and be more at ease with our customers and colleagues? So, what are we waiting for?

Ah… I understand… we're waiting for *them* to be nicer to *us*… then, and only then, will we be nice to them! Is that what's going on? How's that working out?

The thing is, when it's warm and fuzzy, it's not only the other person who benefits. We benefit too. We go home feeling more relaxed having had some lovely conversations all day. That's a lot less stressful. So why not put our ego to one side for one moment and improve it *for ourselves*?

I pointed out earlier in this chapter that we are the professional in the relationship. It's up to us to make it the best it can be. We are there to be *of service*. That's our job.

So, if you are still with me, and you're open to making a change, where would be a good place to begin? Go back to the diagrams. What creates the result? The interaction of the two people. What sets the tone for that? Our *mindset!*

Try this on for size. We meet our 'difficult' customer and we decide to have the same mindset as we do with our 'easy' customer. With that mindset, we have a different attitude and approach to dealing with that customer. We are more helpful. We are curious. We drop our story about the customer. We connect.

Do you think the customer will notice and feel different? Do you think they will respond? Maybe they will start to soften. Not straight away, perhaps. Not every customer, maybe. But is it worth trying?

If you can't bring yourself to do it for the customer, do it for yourself. You deserve to have the best time at work. After all, you spend enough of your life there.

When we are the professional in the relationship (as we all are with our customers) it's necessary to find a way to be at our best, whatever is happening in the rest of our life.

Action tips

- Check your mindset before interacting with any customer or colleague; expect the best and be patient with them – who knows what is going on in their life?
- If a customer or colleague seems 'not OK', use some empathy to communicate caring and understanding
- Choose a few 'difficult' customers and colleagues to win over their hearts – you can do it!

19. MIND YOUR LANGUAGE

You'll recall from Chapter 17 that it's the story we tell ourselves that creates our experience. We all carry stories around with us in our head. Stories about ourselves. Stories about others. Stories about what the world is like. Most of these stories, we never question. 'I'm this way...' or 'I'm that way...', 'They are this way...' or 'They are that way...' and we're on the look out for confirmation that what we believe is actually true.

What we may not realise is that these stories are creating our experience of life. Any story becomes true for us if we believe it. In a perfect way, what we experience provides us with confirmation that what we believe is true.

You may have heard the phrase, 'Speak it into existence'. It's when someone tells a story in advance of it happening. Mohammed Ali decreed, 'I'm the greatest' a very long time before he was. Perhaps you can see the power in this principle. It's the story we tell ourselves that creates our experience.

So, notice the stories that you're not questioning. How it seems is not how it is. There's how something looks to you (through the filters of your story) and there's how it actually is.

Feeling understood

One of the fundamental principles of customer service is for the customer to feel understood. Without this, it can be very difficult to make much progress and the customer often leaves the interaction feeling somewhat underwhelmed.

Let me share with you one of the biggest mistakes I observe some service providers making. It's very obvious to me that they are looking at the world from their own perspective and not from the customer's. What tells me that?

- How often they say 'I', 'me' or 'my'
- How often they talk and don't listen
- How much, when they do speak, they talk about their world rather than the customer's
- Not letting the customer finish speaking
- Not fully acknowledging what the customer has said

Let me give you an example. I was chatting to someone the other day. It wasn't a 'sales' situation but I felt that there could have been business to be done. I was curious. We were in a car together for about 25 minutes. We had a pleasant conversation. When we reached our destination and got out of the car, I noticed that I knew quite a lot about the person I had shared the journey with. I also noticed that he knew nothing about me apart from a few snippets I had offered. What had just occurred?

- I asked many open questions – Chapter 3 (Question)
- I listened carefully
- I asked additional questions to find out more information
- I asked about his feelings
- I asked him about what was important to him
- He asked me no questions
- He seemed to prefer to speak rather than listen
- He seemed to enjoy the experience of talking about his world

This is a really key point. It can be so tempting to transmit to the customer everything we know – especially if we are passionate about what we offer. It's a comfort zone for us. We know what we are talking about. We have a customer to talk to and, boy, they are going to hear it!

You might say 'well, I have to tell the customer about my

product or service'. Yes, that's true. What I'm encouraging you to do is to convey the information in a way that the customer is happy that you not only understand their world but what is important to them and what they trying to achieve.

Another mistake is to 'lose' the customer, leaving them behind in the conversation How do we sometimes do that?

- Using jargon
- Speaking too quickly
- Being too technical
- Giving too much detail when it's not needed
- Not giving enough detail or technical information when it's what the customer really wants and needs to make a purchasing decision

Again, it's about being sensitive to where our customer is at and flexing our approach accordingly. Think about also in the context of how we deal with our colleagues.

Here's a question to ponder. How positive are you? 'Very' I hear you say. Great!

What are some of the ways you like to describe situations, events, and people? When people ask you how you are, do you say 'Not bad'? When you receive a request, do you say 'No problem'? Do you ever say 'I must not forget' or 'I feel tired'? Do you ever place the emphasis on what you don't want? Most people do this some of the time and it's something to watch.

There's a famous story in motor racing about a driver who kept telling himself 'don't hit the wall, don't hit the wall...' Guess what. He crashed into the wall. We create more of what we focus on. *Say what you want to call forth.*

Another famous one is 'Don't think of a pink elephant' – you can try this now if you like – don't think of a pink elephant. What are you thinking about? Exactly – a pink elephant! You can't give your mind the instruction to *not do something* because it makes you focus on it!

- Saying we are 'Not bad' makes us think about being bad;
  Instead, say 'I'm great!'

- Saying 'No problem' makes us focus on problems;
  Instead, say 'Yes, definitely!'

- Saying 'I must not forget' is an invitation to the brain to forget;
  Instead, say 'I must remember' or better still 'I will remember'

- Saying 'I feel tired' makes us feel more tired;
  Instead, say 'I'm looking forward to having a rest'

With our colleagues, we can appreciate them rather than criticise or complain about them. Only speak well of others. You get more of what you focus on.

More about this in Part 3. For now, let's focus on forming the habits of appreciating our customer's perspective and using positive, customer-friendly language as much as possible.

Action tips

- Catch yourself being in your own world. When you notice this happening, switch into 'their perspective' mode
- Match your language and explanations to the customer, avoiding jargon and slang words
- Keep your language focused on what you want to create rather than on what you don't want

---

20. FEEL THE ENERGY

Have you ever hugged a customer? I'm talking about an actual, physical hug. It's possible that you have on at least one occasion but not all your customers, right? How come? How can you tell which customers are open to a hug and which customers are not? Pause to consider your answer for a moment.

I'm guessing that what comes to mind would be phrases like 'I can just tell...' or 'It just feels right sometimes...' What does that mean? How can you tell? Some people would say that it's at times like this we are tapping into our wisdom, our intuition. We are following the energy.

A few years ago, I practiced a martial art called Ki-Aikido. In the Art of Ki-Aikido there is no aggression, tension or competition. Ki means 'Life Force', the natural energy common to all living plants and animals. It is claimed to be a form of energy distinct from that related to pure physical size or muscular strength. Rather, it's something that is around us and within us and that we can tap into at any time. The existence of Ki is a possible explanation for miracle feats - a child is trapped under a car and the mother is able, incredibly, to lift the car to release her child. Something she would not be capable of doing under normal circumstances.

Aikido means 'The Way of Harmony' focusing initially on how to deal effectively with a physical attack. Rather than meeting physical force with force, it's about re-directing and guiding an attack away from ourselves towards the outcome we desire to create. We are trained to use our attacker's energy and force to achieve what we desire.

What I gained from this practice was a deep sense of inner peace and confidence and I learned the ability to feel and use energy.

I can hear you saying 'What has all this got to do with customers?' Think about how some customers have a very strong 'push' energy. They want to take charge and have their needs met. If you meet force with force it rarely ends well, for example deciding to 'block' their energy by saying 'no', or trying to overpower the customer by becoming aggressive or stubborn. On the other hand, we might just decide to 'roll over' which may result in us feeling bad about ourselves or the situation and the customer not respecting us.

There is another way. The Way of Harmony which uses a combination of life-force energy and the other person's energy to achieve an outcome that is good for both.
Here are some suggestions for doing this in a customer service situation:

Connect with the customer energetically.

This may sound weird but it is possible to look beyond the physical person to connect with their nonphysical self. My method is to say in my head 'I love you' (best not to say it out loud). Customers unconsciously feel that energy and respond by letting their barriers down, which causes a deeper sense of connection.

Use your gut, your inner knowing 'I can just tell...' or 'It just feels right sometimes...' Trust it. Follow it. Act on it to find your own way of developing a nonphysical connection.

When a customer (or colleague) is using push energy, remember that we all have everything we need at our disposal to deal with it and that it's not personal.

Be 100% confident. The chances are that the customer is frustrated about something. Use their energy to achieve the outcome that is good for you both. For example, you might avoid confronting their energy, but acknowledging it, aligning yourself with where they are and delicately moving the focus of the conversation away from the negative situation onto what they would like to happen.

I have noticed that customers who bang the table are often the serious buyers; they are not usually there to waste our time. Find a way to help them and make a sale. We can do this by removing or explaining any obstacles to a sale (for example delivery lead times). Most service providers won't know how to deal with this type of customer. The customer will be aware of this; they will have spoken to a few. Maybe that's why they are feeling frustrated. When we show that we are not like most service providers, that we are up to the challenge of dealing with them, the customer will become one of our most loyal advocates.

Action tips

- Develop the ability to 'sense' the customer's energy – then connect with them on this level, beyond their conscious awareness
- Look for the 'Way of Harmony' with every customer – avoid blocking
- Trust your gut feelings, your intuition – this is your wisdom

PLUS ONE – GO FOR GOLD

The brave may not live forever but the cautious do not live at all

Meg Cabot

So, continuing in the spirit of Chapter 10 – 'Do more than expected', here's another bonus chapter!

What gets you out of bed in the morning? Yes, to a very great extent, the need to earn income is forefront in our minds. But there are countless ways to earn income. Why this? What is it about your current work that you enjoy? Knowing *why* you are doing what you do helps you to create more of it.

Rate your enjoyment from your work out of 10 ('1' being virtually none to '10' being impossible to be any better than it is).
Write down your score. below

....
....
....
....
....
....
....

So, as you went through that little mental exercise, what factors came to mind?

I'm guessing that your score probably wasn't '1'. Why not?

What are the aspects that bring you job satisfaction?
What's fun for you? Write them down.

....
....
....
....
....
....
....

Equally, it's unlikely that you rated it a '10' Why not? What
would you like to change about your job? What would make it
more fun? Write that down too.

....
....
....
....
....
....
....
....

Reflect on these lists. They are definitely worth a conversation
with your boss. Yes really! You might actually be surprised at
what is possible (especially if you use some of those Chapter
20 Ki-Aikido tactics on them!)

Why would your boss be interested in helping you to have
more fun and experience greater job satisfaction? Well, some
bosses have worked out that in order to give the customers a
great experience, they need staff members with smiles on their
faces and a spring in their step. Unhappy, demotivated staff
members don't usually deliver a great customer experience!

Not every boss will be turned on to this rocket-science idea, but even without your boss on side there are things you can do for yourself. Talk through your lists with a trusted friend or relative. While you are not expecting them to fix or solve anything, having them listen to you without judgement will be incredibly beneficial in that it will give you much more clarity.

Job satisfaction isn't just about having fun, although it does make a huge contribution. What else is involved? According to the University of Bradford's School of Management, the most important factors that bring job satisfaction include:

- Interesting work
- Job security
- Appreciation of work done
- Good wages
- Promotion and growth
- Loyalty
- Sense of belonging
- Discipline
- Working conditions
- Support

You can do something about some of these factors and some maybe not so much. Identify the most important ones for you (either from the list or add your own) and ask yourself these questions:

- What would it take to have more .... at work?
- What else is possible for me?
- What am I missing here?

....
....
....
....
....
....
....
....
....
....

I asked myself some questions about my career and found that 'Freedom' i.e. 'The ability to control my own destiny' was 'off the scale' important to me - on a par with oxygen! That led to a decision for me to start my own business over 25 years ago. What floats your boat? I encourage you to go on a journey towards creating more of that. Life passes by quickly. It's too short to be someone you're not, but not too short to become the person you always dreamed of becoming.

Action tips

- Identify what is really important to you in your work and make sure you seek plenty of it every day
- Involve your boss, explain the benefits to the business of you being happy in your role
- Ask questions of yourself – What would it take? What else is possible?

PART 3
GUIDE WITH INTEGRITY

Here we are at Part 3 already. How are you feeling about what we have covered so far?

This final part of the book is where we explore how we can add real, tangible value for the customer: how to guide the customer with integrity. Of course, this equally applies to those internal customer relationships too. Passing on to others what we know. It's a huge help to newer members of the team to offer guidance on 'How we do things around here', the team culture, attitude and perspective on things. It's a great opportunity to do a bit of mentoring, something I have personally found to be a great source of satisfaction.

With customers, what puts us in a great place to offer this guidance is having applied what we learned in Parts 1&2 - Handling Skilfully and Understanding Emotionally. Applying these principles will mean that the customer is more likely to trust us and be open to our advice.

Guiding with integrity is about helping customers make the best possible purchasing decisions, ones that they will thank us for, and which will keep them coming back to us in the future.

And these aren't just 'selling skills'. What we are actually covering is a selection of ways to help the customer buy something they would like to have - providing them with valuable information that will help them choose the most suitable product or service for their needs and get the most from it. And I call that 'being of service'.

Tally Ho!

21. ASK

*Develop an interest in life as you see it:
the people, things, literature, music –
the world is so rich, simply throbbing
with rich treasures, beautiful souls and
interesting people. Forget yourself.*

Henry Miller

In Chapter 3 we covered the various kinds of questions we can use in conversations with our customers. It is absolutely essential to use questions to establish the needs of the customer. Without these questions (plus listening to the customer's responses) we are in the dark as to what might be important to the customer, leaving us to make assumptions that could easily be totally incorrect.

So, that's a given. Ask questions. Lots of questions. Not only are they useful in finding out key information, they also have a number of other benefits:

- Questions demonstrate that we are true professionals. Imagine going to see your doctor and even before you have finished explaining your symptoms the doctor begins to write out a prescription. No questions. No examination. That would be malpractice! A true professional spends time investigating what is going on before recommending a solution. Asking questions will result in the customer perceiving you as a professional
- Questions show that we are genuinely interested in the customer and help build rapport. This has a positive

impact on the relationship - we love it when others take an interest in us

- Questions allow us to guide the direction of the conversation. When you watch or listen to an interview you'll notice that it's the interviewer who is in control and that's often because they are following a structure
- Being 'in the question' means we are curious, open-minded and avoid being 'in conclusion', not only about the customer but in life generally!

Ask How They Are Feeling

It's an emotional decision for most people: 'Would I rather have this thing/experience/service... or would I rather have the money?'

Ask the customer how they are feeling about it. Invite them to give you some feedback. Ask them if they have any concerns. If yes, ask (with empathy) 'If those concerns were resolved, would you be happy to go ahead and place an order?'

Ask for the Business

I know that this is a book about customer service. However, one aspect within that is being eager (without being pushy) to win the customer's business. The caveat here is that, before asking for the business, you have laid the foundations by

a. making a positive first impression
b. building great rapport with the customer
c. finding out what's important to them
d. showing them how your product or service will meet their requirements perfectly

If you haven't fulfilled those actions, you're asking too early and that will seem pushy.

To illustrate this point further, you may have experienced going into an establishment where they clearly aren't bothered if you make a purchase or not. That's not Service with a Hug. It's not service at all. Encouraging the customer to say 'yes' is another way of saying 'we really want you to join us and become part of our family'. Don't be afraid. As long as you have done the groundwork, you can ask.

Ask for Referrals and Testimonials

Have you noticed that your best customers tend to send you business through word of mouth? Have you also noticed that those customers are generally a dream to deal with? In my experience, about 20% of customers will give us referrals and recommendations without any prompting. About 20% of customers are unwilling to recommend, no matter how brilliant our service has been. They just won't. That leaves around 60% of our customers who are very willing to recommend us but wouldn't think of it unless prompted to do so. If we ask them, they will no doubt be delighted. So ask!

The alternative to a referral (as described above) is a testimonial. This is an endorsement of the way we looked after them. This can come in the form of a letter, email or online review. Better still if we can capture the customer's warm words on video.

What is it that Stops us from Asking?

Why do we hold back so often? For many of us, it's fear. Fear of hearing the dreaded two-letter word – 'no'. We tend to second-guess what we think the other person will say, and if we don't feel completely confident that it's going to be a 'yes', we don't ask. But how can we be sure if we don't ask? Did anyone ever die from receiving a 'no'? No! But those who ask often get a pleasant surprise and get a 'yes'! I encourage you to be one of those.

Take a risk and... ask!

Action tips

- Ask lots of great questions so that you can give high-value guidance to your customer
- Ask the customer to place the order when it feels like you have recommended the perfect product or service for their needs
- If the customer is happy, ask for a referral, testimonial or review

22. ADD VALUE

Delivering outstanding customer service involves more than superb customer-handling skills and creating positive emotions. Yes, those are really, really important and often sadly lacking in everyday life. However, Service with a HUG also has a reassuring 'consultative' quality.

For instance, the purchase the customer made wasn't the one they anticipated before they had the conversation with you, but as a result of your shedding light on new (to them) information, they made a better, more informed decision. They might (but not always) end up spending a bit more and were happy to do so. Customers feel like they totally made the right decision.

So, how is that done? Here are a few simple, everyday examples of adding value for the customer's benefit:

- In a car dealership parts department, a customer advisor might say 'when replacing your car's radiator, we recommend also replacing the hoses, hose clips and coolant. Would you like me to quote you for those items too?' The advisor goes on to explain the benefits of replacing those items now and how it could save money and inconvenience in the long term
- A supermarket checkout operator might say 'I notice you have only got one of these, they're on offer, 'buy one, get one free'. Would you like another one, free of charge? I'll get a colleague to bring one for you'
- A company that supplies wooden flooring might provide tips and advice on care, what to use to clean the floor, how to deal with any scuffs or scratches, perhaps even including free samples of the recommended products

Focus on Customer Benefits

All too often when I am working with clients, I hear the service teams explaining features and not always the customer benefits. What do we mean by 'features' and what do we mean by 'benefits'?

A 'feature' is some characteristic of the product or service. However, customers don't buy features. They buy benefits. They buy what the product or service will do for them. Explaining the benefits adds huge value for the customer. It helps them to make a more informed choice.

Some time ago, when I purchased my second smartphone, the sales person could have said 'This phone has Touch ID' (a feature) and I would have thought 'So what?' Fortunately, she explained what Touch ID would do for me. She said 'This feature called Touch ID means that you never have to input your unlock code again. All you need to do is place your finger or thumb lightly on the button and it will recognise you, immediately unlocking your phone. It's so much faster, easier and more convenient!' Did you spot the benefits there?

Have a good think about your products and services. Are you talking about features or explaining customer benefits?

Generic benefits vs. personalised benefits

Most products and services have generic benefits – what it will do for you. The main benefit of a power drill is the ease with which it will give you a hole in something.

Taking this to another level, if we know what is important to the customer, we can link our explanation of the benefits to what the customer is trying to achieve.

A personalised benefit, using the example above, would be to explain how a particular power drill is suitable for drilling into the material that the customer wants to make a hole in. Now that's compelling!

Provide Tailored Solutions

Have you ever been to a restaurant when the menu offers all the elements you want, but not all in the same dish? You ask the waiter 'I'd like the salmon, but please can I have it with lentils and spinach?' The waiter says 'Sorry, that's not possible'. You say 'But why not? I don't understand – you clearly have all the ingredients in the kitchen!' Waiter's reply 'No, it's not possible'. So frustrating!

Where do we do that with our customers? I have noticed that the most successful companies are very good at delivering bespoke offerings to customers with a smile - usually because it's an opportunity to charge the customer more. Back to the restaurant example which was really a missed opportunity for them. You didn't ask the price of your preferred combination. You just wanted what you wanted and the restaurant could have charged whatever they felt like for the salmon, lentils and spinach creation. Good for the customer (because they get what they want) and good for the business (because they can charge a premium price). Look at how budget airlines do this: faster boarding, extra legroom, extra bags, extra insurance, etc. It all depends on what is most important to the customer – and the customer gets to choose.

That's my point. Another example of adding value - customers like to be able to choose. So what's possible for you?

....

....

....

....

....

Create Bundles

Almost the opposite of what we have just talked about is the idea of creating a 'bundle' or 'pack' that encourages the customer to buy additional items which offer savings. The supermarkets and fast food outlets do it with their 'meal deals'. Garages do it with their 'service, MOT and valet' packages.

Customers generally like having as much of something as possible, and everybody (generally) likes saving money too. This approach ticks both boxes.

What could you bundle together for your customers?

....
....
....
....
....
....
....
....

Adding Emotional Value

The power of this aspect is not to be underestimated; you'll already know that from reading Part 2. Here's a simple example. As I write this, it's February and I'm in the UK. That means the weather is cold. I live in a rural area and went out for lunch today to a farm shop café. The setting was a converted barn so, it was quite draughty and the heating system was struggling against the sub-zero temperatures outside. The owners of the café were distributing hot water bottles in hand-knitted wool covers to the customers. The feel-good factor of this simple gesture was off the chart. I can honestly say that this was the first time I had ever had that experience. Lunch was wonderful and I will definitely go back there again.

So, it's not the size of the thoughtful gesture, in fact, I believe the smaller the better. It's all about paying attention to the details. Customers expect the big things to be right. It's the small things that separate businesses providing outstanding customer service from the rest. You've heard the phrase 'little things mean a lot' and it's so true. A small gesture can add massive emotional value.

Where could you add emotional value for your customers?

....
....
....
....
....
....
....
....
....
....
....

Action tips

- With each customer, identify ways to add value beyond what they might be expecting
- Make sure that, for each product feature, you explain the customer benefit, tailored to their situation
- For every customer, add emotional value – do something that creates a positive emotion for them

23. RECOMMEND WITH CONVICTION

There's real power in speaking about a product or service from our own experience.

Imagine a customer is shopping around for a vacuum cleaner. They visit one retailer and the assistant says 'Well, there's this one… then talks all about it and there's this one… then talks all about that one and there's this one… and then talks all about third one. The customer asks 'Which one do you find the best?' The assistant says 'I don't really know; I haven't used any of them'.

The customer visits a second retailer and the assistant says 'Let me show you this one… I have used this model myself and what I liked about it was…' Does that have more impact? Which retailer is the customer more likely to buy from? It's obvious!

Well-run restaurants normally hold a 'tasting' session for the staff before they open for business so that the waiting staff are able to speak about every dish on the menu from their own experience.

Many years ago, when I worked in sales at a car dealership, the most frequent question 'What car do you drive?' So I always made a point of driving the same brand of car that I was selling which served me well. Some of my colleagues were driving other brands and when that question came up I saw the look of confusion on the customers' faces as they wondered if they should be buying the other brand!

It's all about demonstrating integrity. I encourage you to experience your products and services. Familiarise yourself with the characteristics, strengths and limitations of each one. Have an opinion based on your findings. Your customers will thank you for your honesty and will come back to you in the future. It's another way of adding value.

If it's impossible for you to try every single one of your products or services, then you can use customer feedback and recommendations. Try saying 'Other customers have found that…' which is also powerful. To be able to do this, ask your current customers how they are getting on. Ask them what they like and what they don't like about products they have bought. You may find that this also deepens your relationship as they will appreciate you taking an interest.

Imagine you go away on holiday. You book through a travel agent. A few days after you get home, the advisor who sold you the holiday rings to ask how you found it. Not a bland 'Was everything OK?', but some specific questions about which aspects of the holiday you enjoyed the most, and anything that didn't work quite so well for you.

If you do this with your customers, not only are you impressing the person who you are calling by demonstrating a high level of customer care but also you are gaining valuable information that you can pass on to other customers.

If it's possible, recommend to the customer that they experience your product or service before buying so that they gain a better sense of what they are buying. Classic examples include:

- Small samples of cheese in a supermarket or farm shop
- A free or reduced-cost weekend in a resort that is selling apartments or timeshare
- Loaning a customer a car of the type they are thinking of buying

- Lending samples of curtains, blinds, carpets, wall coverings, etc. for the customer to see how they work together in the room

When we experience a product, we are far more likely to say yes - assuming that we enjoyed our 'taster'.

How could we give our customers a taster experience of the products or services that we sell?

....
....
....
....
....
....
....
....
....
....
....
....
....

Action tips

- Identify ways of personally sampling the products and services we sell
- Ask customers for their likes and dislikes in relation to any items they have purchased from you
- Find easy ways for your customers to 'try before they buy'

24. KNOW YOUR STRENGTHS

Be Bold, Be Brave, Be YOU

What is it that you do well? Why do your customers love you? What brings you success in your role? Is it your enthusiasm? Your extensive knowledge about the products you offer? The stories you tell? Is it your ability to connect with the customer so that they always enjoy the experience of dealing with you? The way you always, without fail, follow up with customers to make sure they are happy and perhaps offer a further service?

What is it for you?

....
....
....
....
....
....
....
....
....
....
....
....
....
....
....

Almost certainly, whatever you answered, these aspects are your 'USPs', your Unique Selling Points. Customers only get this when they deal with you.

What's the value of knowing our strengths?

- The customer feels confidence in following our advice
- It gives us a platform to build upon in assisting more customers, making more impact in the world and, as a result, becoming more successful
- Even when we encounter a bad situation with a customer, we can feel proud of what we do every day. We may not get it right every time with every customer but we don't need to beat ourselves up about it
- We can let others in our team know what we can (and can't so easily) deliver for them
- We can make better choices in terms of the things we say 'yes' to and the things we say 'no' to

How do we go about finding out more about our USPs?

- Ask our customers 'What do you enjoy most about dealing with me?' and take note of their answers
- Notice what we find effortless, and also what we gain the most enjoyment from doing
- Talk through the list of strengths you wrote above with a trusted friend or family member
- Talk through the same list with your manager and/or your colleagues

One final point -
There's a tendency for us to take our strengths for granted. They are so much a part of being 'us' that they can become invisible to us. This is why it's important to ask others for their perspective, to fill in those blind spots. We sometimes focus on what we are not so good at (e.g. 'I don't do detail') and this thought sometimes undermines our confidence and how we feel about ourselves. We end up comparing our 'weaknesses' with other people's 'strengths'. That's like a tulip comparing itself with a rose and feeling bad because it's not a rose!

Here's my top tip – don't compare yourself to anyone else! Someone I know calls this 'Compare and Despair'! Be proud of who you are. Tell yourself that you *are* enough. Write it large on all the mirrors in your home so that you are constantly reminded. Seriously.

How do we know what is a strength and what is a weakness anyway? It's subjective and depends on what is required in each particular situation. What could be viewed by one person as 'calm under pressure and cool headed' could be seen by someone else as 'emotionally detached, lacking in passion and fire'. The thing to remember is, we are unique in the world and nobody else can offer exactly the same combination of knowledge, skills, experience, stories and personality.

So go forth and confidently offer yourself in service to the world!

Action tips

- Make a list of your strengths and remind yourself regularly that this is what your customers get when they deal with you
- Be aware of your development areas, keep working on those
- Feel good about yourself and avoid comparing yourself with others

25. IDENTIFY HOT BUTTONS

What do we mean by 'hot buttons'? They are what motivate our customer to purchase whatever it is we are offering. These things are sometimes referred to as 'customer needs' or 'buying motives' and they are constantly changing. They affect everything we buy from a bar of chocolate to a new home.

A few years ago, I went to watch an evening football match - a World Cup qualifying game - at Wembley Stadium in London. I went with one of my sons and we travelled there by train – as well as about 90,000 other people. We had an enjoyable time and our team won in convincing style. After the game, it took us a long time to get to Paddington station where we were catching our train home. Except that we didn't. We missed the last train home by less than five minutes.

What were we to do? Stay in a hotel? Or find another way of getting home? Even though it was a journey of around 100 miles, we opted for the second option as we both had work commitments the following morning. We noticed that there were still trains running to Reading which was 40 miles in the right direction. So, we set off, not knowing what would happen beyond Reading.

Once we arrived, we explored options and saw that there was a train going to Didcot, a small town in Oxfordshire that was another 20 miles in the direction of home. The adventure continued! We arrived in Didcot at about 2.00am and took stock of our situation. There were no more trains until about 6.00am. There were no buses. There was no hotel nearby. There was one solitary taxi outside the station. We went to speak to the driver to ask about getting to our home town. Yes, it was possible to take us home but the price quoted was very high. Did we try to negotiate on the price? Actually, yes, I did because that's the way I'm hard-wired! As you can imagine, it was pointless. The taxi driver had no competition and knew we desperately wanted to get home. Our great big hot button was clearly on show! We paid the money and went home to get some sleep.

Customers don't always make it that obvious. However, if we get to know our customer better, understand what has brought them to the point of even speaking to us, they will often be happy to share their hot button. In fact, sometimes they are bursting to tell us! Usually, they just want to deal with someone who will listen and who can suggest a solution. For example, we might be going to a birthday party and need a gift. We may have no idea what to buy as a present. All we want at that moment is to meet a helpful advisor who asks us our budget and shows us a choice of three items so we choose one and wait while the item is gift wrapped (but maybe not how Rowan Atkinson did in the film 'Love Actually').

Once we have identified our customer's hot button or buttons, what does that give us? Before I answer that question, let me give you another example. See if you can answer the question yourself, looking at the situation from the perspective of the customer.

Let's imagine that you're at a music festival. It's Saturday evening and the headline act is expected to start in about 90 minutes. It's cold, raining and muddy (so it's probably in the UK!). It's just getting dark and you didn't pay attention to the weather forecast. Your tent is leaking which has made your bedding wet and you are shivering, dressed as you are in your flip flops, shorts and T-shirt. You are soaked to the skin, cold and feeling miserable. What would you be willing to pay for a hot shower, clean, dry clothes, a thick waterproof jacket, thick woolly socks and wellington boots? Plus a hot meal and a hotel room for later? Probably way beyond what you might normally be willing to pay!

What did you come up with in answer to the question 'What does that give us'?

I would say that when we know the customer's hot buttons, it gives us *leverage.*

What is leverage? According to one definition, *it's the ability to influence in a way that multiplies the outcome of our efforts* (in this case influencing the customer). When our customer really wants their need met, there's not much to do other than to show them something that will do the job. The customer is already feeling motivated; that's why they are talking to us.

Yet it's surprising how often service providers miss these obvious signs and seem to do all they can to stand in the way of the customer getting what they want!

I feel sure that you'll do much better than that...

Action tips

- Develop a 'nose' for sensing the customer's hot button/s
- Match your offer perfectly to the customer's hot button/s
- Remember that the bigger the customer's hot button/s, the more delighted they will be with you for satisfying their desires

26. ANTICIPATE NEEDS

There is a level beyond responsiveness which involves anticipating customer requests and proactively offering before the customer has asked. Think of this as being 'super-helpful'. Imagine the wow that creates for the customer; it's almost like you can read the customer's mind!

When we anticipate our customers' needs, we:

- Demonstrate that we care about our customers
- Reduce complaints (for example if the customer is feeling frustrated about a situation, when we anticipate their needs it can diffuse a situation by acknowledging their feelings, reassuring them that we do actually care)
- Create goodwill
- Sell more (highlighting products or services the customer did not know they needed)
- Create customers who are more loyal

Don't wait for the customer to ask. Anticipate. Seize the opportunity and offer. You'll be amazed at the reaction you get, even from the smallest thoughtful gesture.

I was shopping in my local town shopping centre and had developed a headache. In a small, independent pharmacy, I went up to the counter and asked for paracetamol. As the pharmacist was taking my payment she asked 'Is it to take now?' When I confirmed that it was, she offered to give me a glass of water so that I could take the tablets there and then. What did it cost her? Nothing but a bit of time and the willingness to put herself in my shoes. What was the impact? It was a big 'wow' for me, and I will always recommend that pharmacy, because of that one small, thoughtful act.

I heard a story of someone in a restaurant who was missing an item of cutlery (a spoon) and before she could look around for someone to assist her, a waiter arrived with the spoon that she needed. He had anticipated her need. Impressive, unusual and quite easy if the service provider is paying attention.

A friend of mine used the services of a website specialist after her site had been hacked. The technical wizard was able to carry out the security changes and all was well again. My friend seemed very happy with the cost and her site was back up in no time. A few weeks passed and the website specialist got back in touch with my friend and said that there were further updates that could be carried out to keep the site more secure. My friend was very grateful for the proactive approach and was happy to pay another, very reasonable, invoice. Everyone wins.

We have just looked at examples of what I call 'Low Cost, High Impact' action. What actions could you take in your situation? What merits closer attention? What could you offer that your competitors haven't spotted? Some examples might include:

- Help with children
- Help with shopping or baggage
- Offering refreshments
- Help with parking
- Very clear signage
- Advice/guidance/information
- Confirming arrangements by email/text
- Reminder calls/messages
- Improve waiting times

I have heard many stories over the years of service providers anticipating needs. Often it's the result of paying close attention to what is happening around them. How does the customer seem? A bit stressed? Be curious. What is causing that? What help can we offer?

Sometimes we just need to notice the difficulties that previous customers have encountered and have some extra support available. For example, for a customer setting up a new TV, we could emphasise a particularly tricky or confusing stage in the setup and offer specific advice, offer to be available on our mobile phone to give advice, or even visit the customer's home to assist in person.

Consider how and where you could offer support. It creates a massive wow. It helps more people to become and continue being customers – the lifeblood of any business.

Action tips

- Look for ways to meet unspoken needs that customers might have
- Focus on meeting the immediate needs in the moment and prioritise those actions that have high emotional or personal value
- Investigate 'low cost, high impact' ways to meet the unspoken needs of your customers

---

27. DO YOUR HOMEWORK

True professionals don't just know about their own products and services. They know about the competition's products and services and they know the marketplace. If we are to add real value and guide our customers with genuine integrity, we must know what else customers can buy and how we fit into the overall picture.

That's easy to accomplish these days. The good old Interweb makes it a breeze. There are comparison websites for most things. There are newsletters we can sign up to. Most trades and sectors have their own associations and institutes. There are LinkedIn groups galore. It really is easy to research what's going on. Beyond that, our competitors can be 'mystery shopped'. If you're not familiar with the term, you may have come across the concept of a 'secret shopper'. Why not pretend to be a customer and experience the competition for yourself? What do other businesses do well that we could copy or improve upon? Even if it's not a great experience, never write them off. It might help us to identify areas where our service is lacking. Often when the service is poor, the pricing is aggressive (some rely on low prices to attract customers).

The $64,000 question is: will you make a commitment to take action and do the research?

Admittedly it does take time and effort to stay informed. Average can't be bothered. Outstanding gets into it without thinking twice. Average does the minimum. Outstanding knows that in order to be the best it is part of the game.

Please don't misunderstand me on this. I'm not suggesting that we look for all the weaknesses in the competition so that we can slate them to our customers. Professionals and successful people tend to be gracious about their competitors and speak about them with respect. I've noticed that if we knock the competition, customers tend to defend them. Yet when we speak well of the competition, customers tend to point out all their shortcomings! Sweet!

Doing our research helps us to know our strong points and we can highlight these aspects to our customers. Focus on the positive – always.

What other areas are ripe for homework? (Maybe I should come up with a more appealing name for it! How about homeplay? Answers on a postcard...) How about we do some 'homework' on our customers?

Just for fun, what if we took a really keen interest in their world?

Let's say we have this customer and it turns out they are into canoeing. So, we research canoeing, the clubs and the events that are happening - all that sort of thing. Next time, when the customer comes back, we ask them about their canoeing. Well, at this point, the customer is already blown away by the fact that we remembered anything about them. Now, to totally knock it out of the park, we say to them 'Are you going to the National Canoeing Championships in Nottingham next month?' The look on their face tells us that they are thinking 'how do you know about that?' and that we must be into canoeing ourselves. No, it's not that, it's just our awesomeness showing through!

How great would that feel?

Action tips

- Do some research on your competitors, assess their strengths and weaknesses, see where you score and what you can learn from them
- Sign up for some newsletters, join some associations in your sector
- Get to know more about your customers' hobbies, interests and world

28. WIN

The key to getting ahead is to get started.

Coach Henry Gregory

Most of us like to win, but not at any cost. When two people create an agreement where both sides get what they want, we often refer to this as a win/win. We both feel as if we have had a win and therefore feel happy with the outcome. For example, a customer may get the product or service they want and the supplier generates revenue for the business. This is a great situation and something most of us aim for. But what about a win/win/win?

This is where we create a win/win transaction PLUS we make an investment in the relationship too. Think about relationships as a kind of bank account - when we meet someone for the first time, that's like the opening of the account. The account starts at zero, so we need to make deposits to build up a credit balance.

In relationships, these deposits take the form of small thoughtful gestures starting with being reliable and trustworthy, etc. Every time the other person feels good about us - what we say or do - the balance goes up a little bit. Most people don't keep score, but everyone will have a feeling about the other person based on what has been said and done between them. When something goes wrong, such as forgetting to call when we said we would, it's no big deal as there's plenty in the account. The balance might go down a bit and would eventually run out if these things kept happening. Imagine there was no credit balance built up. What would happen if we let the other person down? Our account would become overdrawn which could lead to a very serious conversation and potentially the end of the relationship.

What about a win/win/win/win? This is a situation where we can create a good outcome for the customer, the business, the relationship and the planet. Truly sustainable agreements do not deplete the earth's resources or cause harm to the environment. This may be an aspect that is not in our control but we can try to do our bit. We can ensure that any packaging or waste is recycled. We can suggest disposal of any discarded products in an environmentally responsible way. We can recommend to the customer the most sustainable solution, for example, if we know that one product will not last beyond a few weeks before it ends up in landfill, while a second option will last a lifetime, we can make the customer aware of the choice they are making and the implications that could result. It's another way of adding value to the customer's decision-making process.

So now, let's go for a win/win/win/win/win! The very best solution is one that benefits everyone – the customer, the business, the relationship, the planet and… us! How do we get to benefit from those daily transactions with customers?

- Perhaps we receive a commission on sales completed
- Perhaps we benefit from repeat purchases made by our regular customers
- Perhaps we are sent a stream of new customers by our loyal customer fan-base
- Perhaps we get to go home with a warm feeling inside after a day of incredible conversations with marvellous customers
- Perhaps we get to become more and more skilful at dealing with customers as each day passes

A word of caution. Some people call their agreements win/win when they are really not. They are actually compromises, for example, 'split the difference' or 'meet me in the middle'. The problem with this type of solution is that neither side is getting what they truly want. Win/win is when both sides get everything they are looking for. That takes time, energy, creativity, determination and a belief that a true win/win is possible. Or even a true win/win/win/win/win.

One final point on 'Looking for the Win'. Larry Gelwix was coach for the Highland Rugby Team for 36 years. In that time, his team recorded 419 wins and only 10 losses. The movie 'Forever Strong' is based on his story. Gelwix came up with W.I.N. as an acronym for 'What's Important Now' which is about making decisions based on what is required of us in this moment. Ignore what just happened. Ignore what the other team is doing right now. The only thing to take all our focus is: What's important now, for us, in this moment?

Action tips

- Look for ways to ensure that what you do always benefits the customer, the business, the relationship, the planet and you
- Keep your awareness in the present moment and keep asking yourself 'What's Important Now?'
- If you don't always feel that you achieved a win/win/win/win/win, it's often impossible to see the bigger picture – trust that everything is working out perfectly!

29. PLAY THE LONG GAME

Have you noticed that when you go to a big city full of tourists (i.e. customers that won't ever be seen again) the service sometimes isn't that great? I'm aware that I've just made a huge generalisation which is unfair to those businesses that do things properly but I'm not talking about them. My point is that delivering outstanding service is about playing the long game.

What do I mean by 'Playing the long game'? Think about what it's like where you work. How would you act differently if it was your business? And what would you expect from those around you? Would you care about the customers more? Would you make more effort? Would you challenge colleagues if they weren't treating customers well? Playing the long game is about considering the future of the business – aspects such as repeat purchase, word-of-mouth recommendations and the reputation of the business out in the world.

Let's not underestimate the power of social media to spread news. It can have a huge impact, as United Airlines found out to their cost. In 2008, musician Dave Carroll claimed that United Airlines damaged his $3,500 guitar during a flight. United failed to reach an agreement with the disgruntled Mr. Carroll and as a result of this dissatisfaction, Dave Carroll composed a song 'United Breaks Guitars'. This was posted on YouTube and attracted half a million views in three days and went on to reach 15 million views by August 2015. United's stock market price fell sharply, costing shareholders $180 million. Had United been playing the long game, they might well have considered the potential impact of not being committed to resolving a customer's complaint. I wish I could say that United had learned from this episode but unfortunately in April 2017 a passenger was forcibly dragged off a United Airlines flight that had been over-booked (by them).

On the other hand, social media can be a very powerful way to spread positive customer service stories. One of my favourites is about Virgin Trains. A passenger on board a UK west-coast express train found himself in the loo without toilet paper. He decided to Tweet Virgin Trains to ask for some. They responded straight away, asking him which coach number he was in. Once they had obtained that vital piece of information, they were able to send a member of staff to the rescue, delivering a fresh supply of toilet paper to the passenger in need. The story was reported in all the national newspapers in the UK and went viral on the internet. A victory for Virgin Trains, who said that they were determined not to let this issue become PooGate!

So, we know that playing the long game is thinking as if we are the owner of the business and are considering the company's wider reputation. What else?

Building a loyal group of customers helps to secure the future of the business. What do we mean when we describe customers as 'loyal'? Is it repeat purchase? No! A repeat purchase might be due to our price or availability being better than another supplier's. As soon as that changes, the customer will be off. That's not loyalty. Loyalty is a customer's desire to do business with a particular supplier, based on how they feel. It's an emotional connection based on trust.

When customers are loyal:

- They purchase from us even if we are not the cheapest supplier
- They recommend us to their friends, relatives and associates
- They are more likely to forgive us when something goes wrong because of all the goodwill we have built up (remember the relationship bank account in the previous chapter?)

- They are more likely to purchase accessories and other add-ons
- They are more likely to use us for other purchases beyond the primary product or service

How do we create loyal customers?

- By ensuring, to the best of our ability, that every purchase the customer makes is the best choice for them, based on what they want it to do (their needs), and NOT based on which product we are trying to shift, or which one has the most profit, or pays us the highest commission. Sure, we could make more profit this time, but it's better to think of the lifetime value of a long-term loyal customer and help them make the best choice for them. That will keep them coming back to us
- By building a strong relationship with every customer, getting to know them well, beyond purely the transaction, remembering facts about them (family members, pets, hobbies, likes, dislikes, etc.)
- By flexing our style of approach to suit each customer individually so that they feel comfortable with us – after all, customers base their purchasing decisions principally on feelings
- By being easy to do business with
- By showing that we care about them

One final suggestion. Obtain customer testimonials and show them to new customers. With these letters, emails, and social media posts we can start to create a sense of community amongst our customers - an unofficial club that new customers will be drawn to and want to be a part of.

Action tips

- Look for opportunities to astound customers – they will do our marketing for us (word-of-mouth, social media, etc)
- Invest in relationships with the customer – remember the lifetime value of every customer
- Care for customers as if it were your own business

30. STAND OUT

People will stare. Make it worth their while.

Harry Winston

One of my biggest passions in life, actually THE biggest passion, is people being who they really are. Yes, being who they REALLY are. In my life, I've found that playing small doesn't serve anyone; especially not ourselves.

In much of my life I've been keeping myself hidden. The real me, that is. Much of this was the result of under-confidence and fear of being judged by others. As I've grown a bit older, I feel that the opinions of other people matter less to me. And actually, much of my head chat wondering 'what will people think of me?' was made up. I was acting as if it was true without questioning it. In my experience, people aren't nearly as interested in my choices in life as they are in their own. You're probably much more interesting, but this principle may apply to you too!

When I'm a customer, I love it when the person I'm dealing with seems connected with who they really are and is prepared to connect with me from that energy. There's something really compelling about it, perhaps because it's not so common.

What would it take for you to bring more of your SELF, your true essence, to your work? What could happen as a result? Not just for you, but for your colleagues and customers too. One of the great things about being more fully ourselves in the world is that it's an invitation and encouragement to others who may feel the urge to express themselves more fully too.

So, what happens when we put this into practice?

- Our customers remember us for the right reasons. We all enjoy telling the occasional 'war story' of how really terrible something was but how often do we tell a story of how amazing the service was? Let's start spreading more stories that feature us being awesome at our jobs
- We eliminate competition – that's because there's only one of us in the world. Even if people can get our product or service elsewhere, we are the unique factor - they can't duplicate us!
- We chip away at all the blandness in the world. Have you noticed how our shopping centres are 90% the same, irrespective of the town or city we happen to be in? The number of independently owned businesses offering a distinctively different range of products seems to be reducing. This can't be a good thing. As customers, we want more choice. We want to buy clothes and shoes and items for our home that enable us to express our own personality. Even if we work in one of the 90% chain stores, we can bring our personality and unique approach to the customer interaction. As the comedian Billy Connolly once said 'Let's eradicate beige-ness'
- As a result of bringing all of the above into the world, we have a more enjoyable and fulfilling life, whether we are the customer or the service provider

I found that once I took a deep breath and started being true to myself, people were able to sense the real me, which made it much easier for us to connect.

Be Brave. Be Bold. Be Who You Really Are.

Action tips

- Take a deep breath and bring your amazing true self to the work you do every day
- Add your own unique personal value to the products and services you offer. The experience of dealing with the real you will make everything more compelling to customers
- Create astounding stories that become legendary in the realm of customer service – see in your mind yourself being held up as a shining example of how it can be done

PLUS ONE – PAY IT FORWARD

Most of the important things in the world have been accomplished by people who have kept on trying when there seemed to be no hope at all.

Dale Carnegie

You may have noticed a recurring theme throughout this book – an invitation to be of service to others, to make a contribution, and make a positive difference in the world. In this final chapter, we take that concept to another level.

One of my favourite movies is 'Pay it Forward' starring Kevin Spacey and Helen Hunt. If you haven't seen it, I thoroughly recommend it. The big idea is that when we are on the receiving end of a good deed or kind gesture from someone else, instead of paying them back (which is transactional), we pay it forward. In other words, we do something for someone else and ask them to pay it forward, thus beginning a chain reaction. A whole movement sprung up after the release of the movie around the concept of selfless giving.

How does this concept apply to you? My goal here is to help you to understand, beyond any shadow of doubt that you really can make a difference in the world far beyond the people and events you interact with personally on a daily basis. You can do something - perhaps a small act of kindness - that changes someone's outlook on the world. Who knows where that could lead? A customer or colleague hugged by you (metaphorically or physically) could lead to them make all sorts of life decisions differently.

Mastering your Life

I've found that it's a good feeling to know about a subject or to possess a certain skill. As I said earlier in the book, I'm a bit of a personal development junkie, passionate about learning and personal growth. My bookshelf is full of positive literature, and that's not counting the books I've passed on to others.

However, I've found that teaching something to someone else is quite a different kettle of fish. When I began my business coaching and facilitating workshops about 25 years ago, I discovered that it requires a much deeper level of understanding and a higher level of skill. In fact, we need to be really living what we teach in order to have any credibility. People spot a fake a mile away.

Therefore, one of the best ways for you to really master the material I'm covering in this book is for you to teach it to others. Not necessarily standing at the front of a training room (but don't rule that out!). No, my challenge to you is to become a customer service champion. A shining example of how it can be done. I encourage you to inspire others through your commitment to excellence.

That doesn't mean just reciting what you have read here. It's inviting you to share your take on it. Describe to others what you have found that works for you in your daily life. Share your stories, your successes, your challenges, and your journey.

It's important to remember that these skills are not just for using at work. They are for every part of your life with your loved ones, friends, neighbours, relatives, the young and not-so-young. They are for you to become a better partner, parent, sibling and member of society. Someone who influences others. Someone who listens to others without judgement and to whom others pay attention. How? You show empathy for how others are feeling. You forgive. You are interested in their world. You are playful and have fun. You take responsibility for the way things are and you are proactive in bringing about positive change. The possibilities for you are infinite.

What could you create?

....
....
....
....
....
....
....
....
....
....
....
....
....

Action tips

- Watch the movie 'Pay it Forward' (watch it again if you have already seen it) and ask yourself what might be possible for you in your daily dealings with customers
- Think of one 'Random Act of Kindness' as you look around you right now. Who could you hug, buy a coffee, pay a compliment or do some other small but potentially life-changing deed?
- When others appreciate your kindness and offer to pay you back, encourage them instead to pay it forward!

THERE'S THE HUG

Wherever there is a human being, there is an opportunity for kindness.

Seneca

Deep down, most people would like a hug. Customers, colleagues, maybe everyone. If you offer one, some people might feel a bit embarrassed and, if so, they'll say 'no'. But deep down many of those people would really like to say 'yes'. Be the change the world needs. Reach out. Take a risk. And don't take it personally if they turn you down – it's nothing to do with you, it's just where they're at in their lives.

Have you heard of 'Global Free Hugs Day'? It's held each year on the first weekend in May. People around the world go into public places - shopping centres and beaches and town squares etc - and hold up signs saying 'Free Hugs'. Many, many people walk past without stopping. Quite a few people stop and accept the free hug being offered. Sometimes it's a very pleasant experience. And sometimes… it's magical. When it is, I'm convinced that another life has been changed for the better. One elderly man said to a member of the 'Free Hugs' group I was a part of 'that's the first hug I've had in 20 years'. It was obvious that he was quite emotional. Sometimes people walk past saying 'no thanks' to the offer of a hug. Then we see them change their mind and come back!

The thought occurred to me that perhaps we need a 'free HUGs for customers' day'. And then I thought that's thinking a bit small! Maybe every day needs to be 'free HUGs for customers' day' – whether that's an actual physical HUG (follow the energy) or a metaphorical HUG by Handling Skilfully, Understanding Emotionally and Guiding with Integrity.

I do hope that you have enjoyed reading this book and that you have found it useful and inspiring. Author and Life Coach Steve Chandler says you read a book once for *information* and twice for *transformation*. It's up to you!

Please stay in touch and share your stories. You can make contact through the website at servicewithahug.com and via social media – the links are on the website.

All the very best on your journey!

ABOUT THE AUTHOR

Andy Collett has delivered training, coaching and consultancy for the past twenty-five years to clients including BMW, Compare the Market, National Grid, Bentley Motors, Whirlpool, Hill Group, Porsche, Apetito, Severn-Trent Water and The London EV Company.

Before that Andy worked in senior management and customer service roles with prestige automotive brands as well as high street retail chains in the UK.

He is passionate about doing business, and life, in a new way – one with fewer rules and greater freedom to express our individuality. He believes that organisations are missing out by insisting that employees conform to a strict set of rules governing how people dress and behave. Andy works with business leaders who support a more open philosophy - those who embrace diversity, encourage a sustainable work/life balance and harness all of the gifts that each individual brings to an organisation.

He lives in rural Wiltshire, UK and enjoys reading, making videos, live performance, clothes and shoes, good food and wine, log fires, walking and being outdoors in nature.
You can stay in touch at servicewithahug.com

www.ingramcontent.com/pod-product-compliance
Lightning Source LLC
Chambersburg PA
CBHW072204290526
45794CB00004B/1646